Social Workers at Risk

The Prevention and Management of Violence

Robert Brown
Stanley Bute
Peter Ford

MACMILLAN

First published 1986 by
THE MACMILLAN PRESS LTD
Houndmills, Basingstoke, Hampshire RG21 2XS
and London
Companies and representatives
throughout the world

ISBN 0–333–37666–8 (hardcover)
ISBN 0–333–37667–6 (paperback)

A catalogue record for this book is available
from the British Library

Printed in Hong Kong

Reprinted 1992

Series Standing Order

If you would like to receive future titles in this series as they are published, you can
make use of our standing order facility. To place a standing order please contact your
bookseller or, in case of difficulty, write to us at the address below with your name
and address and the name of the series. Please state with which title you wish to
begin your standing order. (If you live outside the United Kingdom we may not have
the rights for your area, in which case we will forward your order to the publisher
concerned.)

Customer Services Department, Macmillan Distribution Ltd
Houndmills, Basingstoke, Hampshire RG21 2XS, England

£9.99
NO
Card

PRACTICAL
SOCIAL WORK
Series Editor: Jo Campling

(BASW)

Social work is at an important stage in its development. All professions must be responsive to changing social and economic conditions if they are to meet the needs of those they serve. This series focuses on sound practice and the specific contribution which social workers can make to the well-being of our society in the 1990s.

The British Association of Social Workers has always been conscious of its role in setting guidelines for practice and in seeking to raise professional standards. The conception of the Practical Social Work series arose from a survey of BASW members to discover where they, the practitioners in social work, felt there was the most need for new literature. The response was overwhelming and enthusiastic, and the result is a carefully planned, coherent series of books. The emphasis is firmly on practice, set in a theoretical framework. The books will inform, stimulate and promote discussion, thus adding to the further development of skills and high professional standards. All the authors are practitioners and teachers of social work, representing a wide variety of experience.

JO CAMPLING

Robert Adams *Self-Help, Social Work and Empowerment*

David Anderson *Social Work and Mental Handicap*

Robert Brown, Stanley Bute and Peter Ford *Social Workers at Risk*

Alan Butler and Colin Pritchard *Social Work and Mental Illness*

Roger Clough *Residential Work*

David M. Cooper and David Ball *Social Work and Child Abuse*

Veronica Coulshed *Management in Social Work*

Veronica Couldshed *Social Work Practice: An introduction (2nd edn)*

Paul Daniel and John Wheeler *Social Work and Local Politics*

Peter R. Day *Sociology in Social Work Practice*

Lena Dominelli *Anti-Racist Social Work:A Challenge for White Practitioners and Educators*

Celia Doyle *Working with Abused Children*

Geoff Fimister *Welfare Rights Work in Social Services*

Kathy Ford and Alan Jones *Student Supervision*

Alison Froggatt *Family Work with Elderly People*

Danya Glaser and Stephen Frost *Child Sexual Abuse*

Gill Gorell Barnes *Working with Families*

Jalna Hanmer and Daphne Statham *Women and Social Work:Towards a Woman-Centred Practice*

Tony Jeffs and Mark Smith *Youth Work*

Michael Kerfoot and Alan Butler *Problems of Childhood and Adolescence*

Mary Marshall *Social Work with Old People (2nd edn)*

Paula Nicolson and Rowan Bayne *Applied Psychology for Social Workers (2nd edn)*

Kieran O'Hagan *Crisis Intervention in Social Services*

Michael Oliver *Social Work with Disabled People*

Lisa Parkinson *Separation, Divorce and Families*

Malcolm Payne *Social Care in the Community*

Malcolm Payne *Working in Teams*

John Pitts *Working with Young Offenders*

Michael Preston-Shoot *Effective Groupwork*

Carole R. Smith *Adoption and Fostering: Why and How*

Carole R. Smith *Social Work with the Dying and Bereaved*

Carole R. Smith, Marty T. Lane and Terry Walshe *Child Care and the Courts*

Alan Twelvetrees *Community Work (2nd edn)*

Hilary Walker and Bill Beaumount (eds) *Working with Offenders*

FORTHCOMING TITLES

Jim Barber *Social Work Practice*

Lynne Berry, Crescy Cannan and Karen Lyons *Social Work in Europe*

Suzy Braye and Michael Preston-Shoot *Practising Social Work Law*

Suzy Croft and Peter Beresford *Involving the Consumer*

Angela Everitt, Pauline Hardiker, Jane Littlewood and Audrey Millender *Applied Research for Better Practice*

Michael Freeman *The Children's Act 1989*

Cordelia Grimwood and Ruth Poppleston *Women, Management and Care*

David Hebblewhite and Tom Leckie *Social Work with Addictions*

Paul Henderson and David Francis *Working with Rural Communities*

Rosemary Jefferson and Mike Shooter *Preparing for Practice*

Jeremy Kearney and Dave Evans *A Systems Approach to Social Work*

Joyce Lishman *Communication and Social Work*

Carole Lupton (ed) *Working with Violence*

Graham McBeath and Stephen Webb *The Politics of Social Work*

Steven Shardlow and Mark Doel *Practice: Learning and Teaching*

Gill Stewart and John Stewart *Social Work and Housing*

Contents

Acknowledgements

The authors would like to thank colleagues who have helped in the preparation of this book, especially David Ward and the Research Section Staff at Winchester, and Professor John Martin. The authors and publishers are grateful to the Controller of Her Majesty's Stationery Office for permission to reproduce extracts from the *19th Report* of the Criminal Injuries Compensation Board (1983). We have a particular debt to those who have faced violence themselves, and have been willing to share painful experiences with us. Some are mentioned in the text; we trust that the book does justice to them all.

ROBERT BROWN
STANLEY BUTE
PETER FORD

List of Abbreviations

ACOP	Association of Chief Officers of Probation
ATC	Adult Training Centre
BASW	British Association of Social Workers
CCETSW	Central Council for Education and Training in Social Work
CHE	Community Home with Education
CICB	Criminal Injuries Compensation Board
COHSE	Confederation of Health Service Employees
CQSW	Certificate of Qualification in Social Work
DHSS	Department of Health and Social Security
MH Act	Mental Health Act
NALGO	National and Local Government Officers Association
NAPO	National Association of Probation Officers
NATMH	National Association of Teachers of the Mentally Handicapped
NISW	National Institute for Social Work
SCA	Social Care Association
SEN	State Enrolled Nurse
SSD	Social Services Department

Introduction

This book is about violence towards social work staff. It is concerned with the risks faced by workers in residential, day care and fieldwork settings, in probation, social services and the voluntary sector. It is not about 'working with aggression' as a social work method. Nor is it about violence within families, violence towards people other than social work staff, or violence *by* social work staff towards those in their care, although the second chapter may be relevant to an understanding of violence in general.

The purpose of the book is simply stated: to encourage staff to respond to threatened violence in ways that will minimise risk. It is perhaps a slightly unusual book, in that it contains both research findings and discussion of relevant literature, and yet is not a conventional academic treatise. It is a practical book, stressing good practice and set in a theoretical framework. Because of its subject, it is in places prescriptive to an extent that is uncommon in social work literature, reflecting the authors' consensus about what one should and should not do when faced by someone who is aroused and potentially dangerous. We have tried to make it as clear as possible; before we began, a potential reader told us that 'it would be helpful if it could be put in down-to-earth terms at a level that can be easily assimilated without the need for unnecessary jargon, sometimes misunderstood to be a necessary part of professionalism.' We have striven to observe this dictum.

In July 1978 a Hampshire social worker, Mr Peter Gray, died while visiting a deaf and dumb client, who was subsequently made the subject of a hospital order after he had been diagnosed as suffering from paranoid psychosis. This tragedy led one of the authors, Stanley Bute, of Hampshire Social Services Department, to undertake a study of violence towards social work staff, under Bristol University's Personal Fellowship scheme. He went on to produce a booklet of guidelines for staff on the management of violence. The heavy demand for this booklet encouraged the three of us to produce a training package on the subject, comprising a short video film and accompanying booklet. This also sold well, convincing us of the demand for such training materials, and led in turn to the suggestion of this book.

Our discussions with numerous social services and probation staff in different work settings indicated that many of them had faced violence, threatened or actual, during their careers, as we ourselves had done. It seemed to us that it would be worth trying to produce a book that would help staff to bridge the gap between the classic psychological studies of aggression and the daily realities of social work. Our collective experience includes practice in probation, social services, mental health and community work, and further experience in social work management and training.

The book is offered to a wide range of staff, including field social workers, probation officers, line managers, receptionists, telephonists, staff in day centres, homes, hostels and institutions, lecturers, trainers and students. Some chapters, such as the final one which is concerned with training, have particular relevance for part of this audience, but others, such as the second one, 'Understanding Violence', are intended for everyone. The theme of the book is the prevention of violence by the adoption of good practice. Linked to this is the notion that social work staff seem to handle the majority of threatening incidents with confidence and ability; however, the practical skills used in handling aggression are very rarely discussed and shared with others.

The first chapter is addressed to a widespread ignorance of the extent of violence towards staff in social work agencies, including fieldwork, residential and day care settings. It is based on some hitherto unpublished data from a survey carried out in 1979, and although the sample of 338 replies contains some degree of bias, we give it prominence because it provides detailed indications of the hidden problems of violence in social work agencies in one area of the United Kingdom. The second chapter introduces a range of psychoanalytic and behavioural theories relevant to an understanding of aggressive behaviour. It is followed by a set of four chapters which deal with recognising potential violence, preventing it from happening, responding appropriately if violence nevertheless occurs, and obtaining help and support after an incident. Each of these chapters concludes with a summary of 'Points for practice'. Chapter 7 explores issues for social work managers in a range of different settings, and includes a 'Checklist for Managers'. The book ends with some practical suggestions for training.

Our examination of the violence experienced by social work staff raises some interesting questions. In a recent unpublished lecture, Professor Percy Cohen of London University discussed the sociological aspects of social control. He argued that centralised states often have marginal groups at their frontiers, and that the imposition of state control generates violence both to and from the agents of the state. It seems to us that this point applies not only to terrorists in the Basque region or Northern Ireland, but also to social workers who have the duty of implementing laws concerned with the welfare of children, the old and the mentally ill. The removal of people from their homes to institutions is associated with particular risks to staff, as we shall see later in this book.

Violence is exciting, sensational and frightening; it would have been relatively easy to illustrate this book with pictures that excite and frighten, but we have tried not to be sensational. Illustrations from experience have been included because they serve to highlight the details of good practice. Perhaps the most important of all the comments made to us as we prepared the book came from a group of young people resident in a local probation hostel, some with convictions for violence. Whatever you do, they told us, do not upset our relationships with the staff; the last thing they wanted was to be categorised as violent, and for staff to retreat behind a barrier of suspicion and fear. They gave us an unexpected and salutary reminder of the continuing importance of traditional social work relationships, and nothing we say in the following chapters should detract from their point.

1

How Widespread is Violence?

Violence towards social workers has been researched more
systematically in the USA than here in the UK. However, in
this chapter we are able to include some previously unpublished data from a postal survey which was carried out in 1979 in
Wessex. After we have examined the results of this survey we
will review briefly some of the American studies.

The Wessex Study

A questionnaire was sent to 560 staff working in the personal
social services in Wessex. They were contacted through
professional organisations. Most were employed by one of
three local authorities. The 338 people who replied gave
information which indicated: the number of times they had
been the victims of violence, or threats of violence, in the
preceding three years; the setting in which they worked; their
age, sex, qualifications and years of experience; the client
group they worked most with and how much direct contact
they had; their views on violence and level of concern with it
compared with other issues; their attitude to guidelines and
training; details of the most recent violent incident which had
involved them. Violence to the person was defined as actual
physical assault resulting in some injury or pain, while violence
to property involved some actual damage.

As we have seen the sample was not random, consisting of
members of several professional organisations within the
Wessex region. One example of the bias resulting from this
approach was that most of the 44 day care respondents worked

in the mental handicap field. It is also possible that the 60 per cent who sent in replies were more likely to have been victims of violence than the 40 per cent who did not reply. Despite this the level of violence indicated was higher than had been expected. Respondents were asked how many times in the last three years of their current (or last) post they had been subjected to actual violence or threats of violence, and how many times their families, close friends or possessions had been subjected to violence by clients. 180 people (53 per cent of the total) had been victims in at least one of these ways. 98 people (29 per cent) had actually been physically assaulted at least once and 62 of these (18 per cent of the total) had been assaulted more than once. 134 people (40 per cent) had been threatened at least once and 102 of these (30 per cent of the total) had been threatened more than once in the preceding three years.

These figures can be broken down to show the incidence for residential, day care and fieldwork staff. Where staff were clearly in administrative posts (for instance advisory/ headquarters posts) they were categorised separately and this accounted for twenty respondents. Where the workbase was unclear or did not fit the main categories (for instance academic staff) respondents were put in an 'other' category and this accounted for twenty-one people. Five gave no indication at all of their workbase. This meant that there were: 177 fieldworkers, 71 residential workers, 44 day care workers. These three groups of respondents form the basis for the discussion which follows. It should be noted that receptionists were not included in the Wessex study although as 'front line' workers they are affected by many of the same issues as the respondents.

Violence towards fieldworkers

There is a danger in looking at violence within the three conventional divisions of residential work, day centre work and field work, that general comments may be considered to apply solely to those working in one of the three types of setting, excluding workers from the other two groupings. This is not our intention. We seek only to point out that some common types of situation may occur which are at least partly a function of the work setting.

When we seek to define 'fieldwork', the problem of finding a common element is especially acute. In the Wessex study, the following groups were deemed to be fieldworkers:

(i) staff based in social services area teams (social workers, home help organisers and so on);
(ii) staff working from hospitals or clinics (virtually all of whom were social workers);
(iii) probation officers (other than those based primarily in residential or day centres);
(iv) other workers visiting clients from an office base.

Nearly all the respondents classified as fieldworkers came from one of the first two groups and were employed by the local authority (164 out of 177). However this does not really make the group much more homogeneous than if more probation officers and others had been included. An examination of 'what social workers in field settings do' in the Barclay Report contrasts the work of an area team social worker with that of a hospital social worker (Barclay, 1982, ch. 1). The settings may be quite different, but there were similarities in the tasks undertaken. The balance between counselling, negotiating, mediating, planning and so on would vary according to the setting and the level of staffing, but they were still common elements, and one would expect to find them repeated for probation officers and others. Thus we would expect some common elements in the work but equally some significant variations. In drawing any general conclusions, this should be borne in mind.

The influence of 'genericism' on workloads was still fairly strong in the area studied, and 53 per cent had mixed workloads with no clear specialism. Of the respondents who could identify a clear specialism, those working with children were the biggest group (17 per cent) followed by those working with the elderly (7 per cent) and those working with the mentally ill (6 per cent). The remaining 17 per cent included a range of specialisms and others who did not describe their workload in sufficient detail.

The level of violence

The level of personal violence against fieldworkers was lower than for those in residential or day care settings, as can be seen from Table 1.1. However, it still emerged that 22 per cent had been subjected to actual physical violence within the previous three years of their current post. The fact that only the current post was counted may have led to a slight understatement of the level of violence for this group, because 35 per cent had been in their post for a year or less compared with 27 per cent of residential workers and 19 per cent of day care workers. On the other hand, it might be that fieldworkers are more likely to remember and record violent incidents in such a study, because of the fact that they occur in more public settings in the sense that they are not so frequently on agency property. When we

Table 1.1 *Staff in various settings with experience of at least one violent incident in previous 3 years of current post.*

	Number of staff assaulted	Number of staff in sample	% assaulted
Day centre	22	44	50%
Residential	32	71	45%
Field	39	177	22%
Other	5	21	24%
Administrative	0	20	0%
Total	98	333	29%

look at threats of personal violence, the figures are similar for fieldworkers (43 per cent) residential workers (45 per cent) and day care workers (39 per cent). Some of the threats to fieldworkers were particularly serious, and we will give some examples in the next section. Finally, 12 per cent had had possessions damaged by clients, and this was in line with the average for all respondents (13 per cent).

The violent incidents

The relatively large sample of fieldworkers (177) made it possible to draw conclusions about the types of incidents that had occurred, and some significant patterns emerged. Of the detailed incidents (the most recent for each respondent), 42 per cent had occurred in the client's home, 19 per cent in an office and 11 per cent in a car or ambulance while escorting a client to hospital or residential establishment. All three of these are situations where the worker may not have any colleagues immediately available, and this was a surprisingly common feature. Two of the more tragic incidents of recent years, the death of Peter Gray in 1978 while visiting a client's home and the death of Isobel Schwarz in 1984 while working alone in her hospital office, serve as reminders of the risks involved in working alone. This may frequently be an unavoidable risk, but on other occasions it may be possible to reduce it and we shall consider this further in a later chapter in the context of issues for managers.

When we look for common precipitating factors in the fieldwork sample, two major groups emerge. Both types of incident involve the deprivation of personal liberty, and the theme of social control is one to which we shall return. The first group concerns children being taken into care, and the second group concerns the compulsory admission of mentally disordered persons. Of the recorded incidents, the first group accounted for 26 per cent and the second for 30 per cent. Other identifiable precipitating factors were: withholding information or services – 10 per cent; giving advice or disciplining a client in a residential home or day centre – 9 per cent; intervening to protect a third party from injury – 3 per cent. These figures are quite different from those which applied for residential and day care staff, where the last two types of situation accounted for well over half of the incidents. In fieldwork they only accounted for 12 per cent. This must be remembered in policy making and in the planning of training.

Deprivation of liberty – child care

There were several vivid illustrations given by respondents which bear some examination. The first combines a typical conflict over child care with a demonstration of why threats can often have a serious effect on the worker. 'Place of Safety order on 13 year old son. Father verbally threatened me and told other people present that he was going to shoot me with a

shotgun which was always visible in the corner of the living
.room . . .'

The second child care example raises the question of whether
or not consideration was given to the worker being accompanied on the home visit, given the nature of the task.

> Necessity to be completely frank and explain probability of application
> for parental rights . . . client verbally extremely aggressive. Boyfriend
> returned from shops . . . both made clear their intention to do me in if
> parental rights taken. Mother coldly stated she'd probably kill me and
> wouldn't care about consequences. Boyfriend extremely physical and
> amidst threats manhandled me from premises.

The social worker may often be seen as the symbol of
authority, or the individual responsible for the removal of the
child, or just a convenient target for aggression when frustration over loss of control over one's child reaches boiling point.

The final child care example involving a parent is selected to
re-emphasise the point that some situations are known in
advance to contain elements of conflict, making the worker
especially vulnerable and perhaps suggesting a need for the
presence of a second worker.

> In a family home, when I was discussing care proceedings, with a mother
> and her cohabitee, of her 10 year old female child who had previously been
> subject to a place of safety order. At a crucial and delicate part of the
> discussion the cohabitee threw a freshly made cup of hot coffee over me
> and pushed me backwards down the hallway and out of the door. I was
> treated for bruises, scalds and shock.

There were several reported incidents involving children
themselves, and these occurred mainly during journeys to and
from residential establishments rather than in homes or at
home. They ranged from serious physical assaults to 'small boy
kicked the inside of my car while being taken into care. No
damage done. I was not cross with him.'

Deprivation of liberty – mental health

The other major group of events concerned compulsory
admissions to psychiatric hospital. The following was typical

of the responses: 'Visit to psychiatric client to assess for compulsory admission to psychiatric hospital. Was pushed off the chair to the floor, shaken and received blows on shoulder and head.' It was noticeable that social workers were much more likely than not to be accompanied by other staff (police, ambulancemen and so on) to the point where sometimes this might be considered excessive and possibly provocative. 'Whilst completing a section 26 [MH Act 1959] on a client. A lady I had known for 7 months. I was hit on the head by a large book. This occurred in her house, the injury hurt. Because of her aggression there were four police constables assisting, this may well have helped precipitate her actions.'

A consistent problem for social workers involved in potential compulsory admissions to psychiatric hospital is the decision of whether or when to call for the assistance of the police, ambulance service or other colleagues. Once a decision to make an application has been made, the possibility exists of having to use physical restraint, both to effect the admission and as a protection against violence from the patient. In contrast with many other situations, the first physical move is often made by the social worker, in leading the patient towards the car or ambulance. In any event the timing of the arrival of assistance can be crucial, as in the following example: 'Threatened with violence by mentally ill client during compulsory admission. He then ran off and threw a brick at me, screaming. In restraining him we both fell to the floor in the street. Ambulance arrived and with assistance of driver client was admitted to hospital.'

There were several examples of a decision being reached which was then conveyed to the patient, who reacted violently. Where transport assistance was delayed, severe difficulties could occur, and the following was a typical example:

Location in client's own home. She was an elderly woman, over 80, but as strong as a horse. She had been sectioned under the MH Act and we were waiting for an ambulance which was delayed. A female community nurse was with me. Client had practically to be sat on to control her. She grabbed my glasses, spat on me and scratched my arm. I am sure fear of hospital drove her to this outburst.

The advisability of having at least one colleague present was clear in this case, as in many others.

It is probable that section 135 of the Mental Health Act 1983 (obtaining a warrant to search for and remove patients) is underused. David Carson has questioned the legality of those assessments for compulsory admission where the patient who lives alone has clearly told the social worker not to enter, or has instructed them to leave the premises, and as Carson put it 'occupiers not wishing to be detained are likely to wish to expel those with the power to do so' (Carson, 1983, p. 201). The obtaining of a warrant in such circumstances necessitates the presence of the constable named in the warrant and a doctor, and such support may sometimes be appropriate, although there are examples of excessive numbers of people being involved.

Even when assistance is at hand, the process of assessing the possibility of detention in a psychiatric hospital is one of high risk. The following example occurred within the hospital itself: 'Spectacles broken by client whom I was interviewing in a psychiatric hospital ward with a view to an application under section 26 of the MH Act 1959. Glasses snatched from my face and frame broken in half. Client manic at the time and refusing all medication.'

Other incidents

Although issues to do with the deprivation of liberty (of children and of mentally disordered adults) accounted for 56 per cent of all incidents recorded in detail, there were other examples which bore some similarity to those in residential and day care settings, where the worker was advising or disciplining the client, or was intervening to protect a third party from injury. For example, one worker had to intervene to protect a girl from her father during an interview. More common were examples where the worker had to give information about a service not being available: 'Interviewing no fixed abode client as daytime duty officer in interview room in area office. My refusal to give cash precipitated client throwing an armchair. Dodged chair and left room.' The office setting is clearly of some relevance in this type of situation, as the next example indicates: 'Aggressive patient of no fixed abode demanding money. Got abusive and aggressive when not forthcoming. Seen in office away from main building and no means of exit between myself and client. Finally left when I used telephone to call porter to remove him.' Reception arrangements and offices layout are considered in Chapter 4.

There were a few home help organisers among the respondents, and several gave instances of violence or threats due on many occasions to mental disorder or confusion. Several others were triggered by the withdrawal of services or the inability to provide more; for instance, 'elderly gentleman shouting abuse and waving his walking stick at me because he was demanding more home help service'. Home helps were not included in the survey although several home help organisers stated that they were more likely to be the victims of violence than were the organisers themselves. They also stated that the home helps needed more in the way of training and support.

Staffing, pay, and other areas of concern

Pay and conditions may have improved to some degree in the past ten years, but they are still relevant considerations in any discussion of factors contributing to violence. In the Wessex study, people were asked to compare their concern about the possibility of violence by clients with their handling of a particular case, publicity following inappropriate action, accountability for professional action, staffing levels in their organisation and pay and conditions of service.

Fieldwork staff were slightly more concerned with the level of staffing in their office than with the possibility of violence by clients, and slightly less concerned with pay and conditions of service. Where they were most at odds with the views of residential and day care staff was in their much greater concern with publicity following inappropriate action and with their accountability for professional action. They also had a more clear cut concern with how they had handled a particular case. These attitudes may be connected with press coverage of the role social workers had played in various child care tragedies that had led to enquiries. They could also reflect the fact that incidents often occurred in public places rather than on agency property. Another issue raised by respondents was the poor support received by the worker after a serious incident. This point has been repeated in training sessions that we have run and would appear to be a common problem.

Guidelines

Fieldworkers in this study were more likely to hold a relevant qualification (89 per cent) than either day care workers (73 per cent) or residential staff (56 per cent). However, whether this had been basic training or in-service training, fieldworkers were far less likely to have been given any guidance in the practical management of violence. Only 14 per cent (or roughly one in seven) had been given any such training at any point in their careers.

85 per cent of the fieldworkers thought that there should be printed guidelines for the management of violence (although their faith in them was not as great as the administrative workers, of whom 95 per cent took this view). This is still a high figure and again, although it was generally thought to be the employer's responsibility to provide guidelines, at the time of the study very few employers actually did so.

As with the other two main staff groups, there was an overwhelming majority in favour of including legal advice on physical restraint in guidelines (97 per cent) and in any in-service training (92 per cent). There was some difference, however, on the question of including advice on techniques of physical restraint. There was still a clear majority (77 per cent) in favour of including this advice in guidelines, but the figure for residential staff had been much higher (95 per cent), as it had for day care staff (92 per cent). The same point applies for attitudes to the inclusion of advice on techniques of physical restraint as part of in-service training, where the figures were: fieldwork staff (76 per cent), residential staff (96 per cent), day care staff (90 per cent). These results may reflect the fact that fieldworkers in many situations would be more concerned with escape than with restraint. There would be little point in using restraint if the worker was in the client's home and had no colleagues at hand to assist.

Violence towards residential workers

Residential workers accounted for 71 of the 338 respondents to the Wessex study and 64 of them were employed as such when they completed their questionnaires. The majority, 56, worked (or had worked when employed) for the local authority. They covered different client groups as follows: 39 worked with children, 14 with the elderly, 4 with the mentally handicapped, and the rest worked with other groups or did not specify where they worked. 44 of the residential staff were women and 27 were men. 45 per cent of the residential workers had been attacked at least once in the previous three years, while 32 per cent of the residential workers had been attacked more than once in the previous three years. The study did not allow comparisons between establishments to be made to see, for example, if in similar establishments those with more male staff had a higher level of reported violent incidents. This may have been the case, because, of the *total* group of respondents (338), 39 per cent of the men had been attacked at least once in the previous three years, while for the same period 22 per cent of the women had been attacked. An attack is defined here as an actual physical assault on the person and some examples are given in the next section.

Some had been attacked more frequently, so that of the total group, 28 per cent of the men had been attacked more than once in the previous three years while only 12 per cent of the women had been attacked more than once.

Apart from their sex, there were certain characteristics of the residential staff in the sample that might have some relevance, although none by itself explains the high level of violence. There were more under the age of twenty-five than in the total group, and the incidence of violence for the under twenty-fives in the total group was above average. Residential workers were much more likely to be working with children than any of the other groups. Not surprisingly, the amount of direct contact with clients was higher than for the fieldworker group, and it was lower than for the day care workers. This is one possible explanation for the fact that day care staff suffered from the highest level of violence.

Residential staff were less likely to have a professional qualification (56 per cent) than day care (73 per cent) or fieldwork staff (89 per cent). Even where they had been trained, this rarely included advice on the prevention or management of violence, so that the impact of training was probably very small. This is an area in which some remedies can be found.

The study looked beyond those incidents where the worker had actually been subjected to physical violence. Threats of physical violence can be very potent. 45 per cent of the residential workers had been threatened with physical violence in the previous three years, and this was a little higher than the figure of 40 per cent for the total group. Before we look at some of the incidents of actual and threatened violence, it is worth noting that there was a higher risk of damage to staff possessions in residential care than in any of the other groups. 21 per cent of the residential staff had had possessions damaged by clients, whilst for other groups the corresponding figures were: fieldworkers (12 per cent), day care staff (7 per cent), administrative staff (0 per cent), other staff (10 per cent).

The violent incidents

Some data were gathered about the violent incidents themselves. Respondents were asked to record details of the most recent incident and, before we look at various case examples, some of the common factors can be itemised. The majority of incidents took place in the residential home itself but, perhaps surprisingly, 20 per cent took place elsewhere (for example in the client's own home or at a day centre). Precipitating or 'trigger' factors are hard to classify, but over half the recorded incidents in residential care involved the members of staff giving advice, disciplining the client or intervening to protect a third party from injury.

An example of this last type of incident was described by one of the respondents:

A sixteen year old returned to the home drunk the day before he was due to leave after being in the home for three to four years. He tried to attack a young boy. I tried to stop him and he tried to strangle me then punched me twenty times because I wouldn't let him 'do over' the other boy. He cracked my nose and in the end the police had to stop him.

Given the staff member's duty to provide care for the residents, it is hard to see how they could have avoided some violence in this situation. One hopes that the incident was discussed fully in the staff group afterwards and we shall consider the need to evaluate incidents later.

Care and control are common concerns for social services staff, and their part in the thought processes of a member of staff involved in a violent event are apparent in the comments of another respondent on their most recent incident: 'Control of highly disturbed adolescent boy within the children's home. Required self defence and chose physical restraint. The priority being to prevent self injury to the boy or the boy injuring a member of staff or third party. Force applied and isolated to ensure above conditions.'

There were relatively few respondents working in residential homes for elderly people, but it is clear from those who did reply and from subsequent discussions with workers in such establishments that the level of violence in many homes is high enough to cause considerable concern.

One view that we have been given is that there are so many incidents in this setting that the majority would be considered by staff themselves to be relatively unimportant, witness the following example: 'In an old man's bedroom when he did not wish to be bathed. Started threatening. Started whirling his arms windmill fashion. Went to grab his stick but I moved it. Ripped pocket of my shirt.' It is not safe, however, to say that such incidents are not worth reporting. It is very important for management to know that they occur and to facilitate discussion on how they might be handled or, preferably, avoided, along with the many other more serious incidents.

One senior member of staff in the residential sector showed an awareness of these issues in a detailed letter which will sound familiar to many of those working with the elderly in local authority homes. The writer expressed particular concern for junior members of staff, who have the most face to face contact with residents but are not always equipped to deal with violence when it occurs.

It is often after the resident has calmed down before the care assistant can contact the senior staff on duty . . . we have had several violent and aggressive outbursts recently, one when a chair was raised by an octogenarian resident above his head and smashed over the care assistant's head causing a blow to the shoulders as the staff member ducked. On another occasion a resident kicked a male member of staff in the groin violently. These incidents have become more frequent due to a change in the type of residents being admitted. The residents are usually in a mentally confused state, getting up in the middle of night and wandering into other residents' rooms. The occupier of the room resents the intrusion and tells the intruder to get out, at which the intruder immediately becomes aggressive and agitated. Then the care staff become involved and deal with the situation immediately.

The writer goes on to argue for training and support for staff in how to cope with different forms of behaviour problems, and to ensure that staff know their legal position, opinions with which we concur.

Other areas of concern

Residential workers were more concerned with violence by clients than with publicity following inappropriate action or with accountability for professional actions. These responses were similar to those of day care staff, but in marked contrast to fieldworkers, who may have become sensitised to these issues by a series of public enquiries which had occurred before the survey was carried out.

Residential workers were more concerned with their own handling of a particular case, and even more so with the level of staffing. The potential connection between poor staffing levels and violent episodes is fairly obvious, for example staff being unable to call quickly for assistance, but it is remarkably underexplored in social services and probation settings. Readers may find some interesting parallels, however, in John Martin's recent study of inquiries into hospital care. He found that understaffing was the most common explanation given for 'scandals' or bad conditions over the last twenty years, but that this was by no means the sole explanation (Martin, 1984, p. 222). Returning to the Wessex study, residential workers regarded pay and conditions of service as of identical importance to their concern with violence by clients. However, some respondents added a note that they were particularly concerned with the risk of violence from one resident towards another, and how they should handle such situations, and this concern has been reiterated in subsequent discussion with colleagues in residential settings.

Guidelines and training

Only a quarter of the residential workers had received any guidance in the management of violence as part of any vocational training (including 'in-service' and 'on the job' training) they had undertaken. It is worth noting, however, that the position for fieldworkers was even worse, with only one in seven workers having received guidance on the management of violence. 90 per cent of the residential workers felt it necessary to have printed guidelines concerned with the management of violence, and the commonly held view was that this should be the responsibility of the employer, although a few people suggested that the DHSS or CCETSW should take a lead. Given the role that COHSE had already played in producing its guidelines on 'The Management of Violent or Potentially Violent Patients' (1977) it is perhaps surprising that only one person considered that this should be a responsibility mainly for the trade unions, although it should be noted that COHSE produced its guidelines as a protest against the inadequacy of those drawn up by the DHSS.

In the Wessex study, when asked about the content of guidelines 98 per cent thought that they should include advice on the law as far as physical restraint was concerned, and 95 per cent thought that they should also include advice on techniques of physical restraint. These findings add significance to our discussion of restraint in Chapter 5.

Finally in this section, a letter from a worker in a girls' residential home gives one view on how to reduce the possibility of violence occurring:

In my 15 years experience working with teenagers I have never experienced violence against staff. I believe this is because:
1. It is made clear from the beginning that violence is not acceptable either in the group or against staff – it only leads to further trouble and is therefore wasted energy.
2. Every child is respected as an individual and is treated as such.
3. A personal weekly opportunity (is given) to air grievances . . . in

private or in the weekly group meeting where all girls and staff are present.
4. Time is always given to listening to a child when this is required.

Violence towards day care workers

Day centres in their various forms have been a growth area over the last ten years. The push for 'community care' and the development of new ways of working have been two factors that have contributed to this process, and there have been changes in health service provision as well as in probation, social services and the voluntary sector.

As we shall see later, the *regime* has a crucial influence on the level of violence. This is more important for day care workers than for fieldworkers in relation to violence, in that most incidents (and of course most contact) involving day care workers take place within the centre itself. Only 44 of the 338 respondents were identified as day centre workers and, as we shall see, most of them worked in Adult Training Centres (ATCs) for the mentally handicapped. Their replies were detailed and made some important points. A similar study with a greater focus on day centres might yield further insights, especially as the level of personal violence against day centre staff was higher than for any of the other groups studied, as Tabel 1.1 (above) indicated. Within the group who had been personally assaulted, the majority of day care staff had been assaulted on more than one occasion. This meant that 34 per cent of all day centre respondents had been personally subjected to actual violence on two or more occasions within the three year period.

Given the level of violence reported in this study, it should be noted that in the limited but growing literature on day centres, very little attention has been given to the problem of violence. 41 of the 44 respondents worked in local authority day centres and the other three worked for the NHS. 30 worked with mentally handicapped adults in ATCs and the remaining 14 worked with a range of other client groups. Whether ATCs are especially prone to violence is debatable, and the numbers working in any other single type of day centre in this study were too small for any significance to be attached to them.

We noted earlier that violence occurs more fequently to men than to women. Day centres had the highest proportion of men in the sample. 54 per cent of the day centre respondents were men, compared with 36 per cent for the combined groups. However we do not regard this as the only factor contributing to the high level of violence. Equally important is the amount of time spent in direct contact with clients. Workers were asked how much of their time was spent in contact with clients and the results are given in Table 1.2, which compares contact with the amount of violence. Thus a clear picture developed which

Table 1.2 *The relationship between the amount of client contact and the number of personal assaults on staff*

Frequency of contact	Total number	Number in this group personally assaulted	% assaulted
Rare	28	4	14%
Some of the time	111	23	21%
Most of the time	194	71	37%

was common to all workbases, that the likelihood of being physically assaulted increased with more client contact. An examination of the different workbases then showed that the amount of contact was highest in day centres, where the level of violence was also highest (see Table 1.3).

Table 1.3 *Staff contact with clients (% in brackets)*

Workbase	Total in group	Number rarely in contact	In contact some of the time	In contact most of the time
Day Centre	44 (100%)	1 (2%)	3 (7%)	40 (91%)
Residential	71 (100%)	1 (1%)	13 (18%)	57 (80%)
Field	176 (100%)	14 (8%)	80 (46%)	82 (46%)
Other	20 (100%)	3 (15%)	8 (40%)	9 (45%)
Administrative	20 (100%)	9 (45%)	7 (35%)	4 (20%)
Total	331 (100%)	28	111	192

While there are dangers in making generalisations from a small and biased sample, the pattern of more violence being associated with more contact does seem to be consistent throughout the study and in our subsequent interviews with staff from various settings. The results would suggest then that men working in close contact with clients in day centres are the most likely group to be assaulted, and that some priority should be accorded to dealing with this problem.

The violent incidents

The link between maintaining control and the level of violence was especially apparent in an examination of the incidents reported by day care workers. Of those incidents reported in any detail, 62 per cent clearly indicated that the main factor precipitating violence was either the member of staff advising or disciplining the client, or intervening to protect a third party from injury. One example was a heavy blow to the head received by an instructor in an adult training centre when he reprimanded a trainee for running in the dining hall. A similar example, but where violence was threatened rather than actually used, was reported thus: 'I was offering some advice regarding smoking in workshop areas to a trainee . . . [who] would not accept advice and threatened to fill me in after working when he said he would be waiting for me.'

One explanation for violence put forward by a victim of an assault in an ATC was that the policy of including some mentally disturbed trainees with others who were mentally handicapped created extra difficulties. It is hard to see how this problem could be completely resolved when we know that some mentally handicapped people will inevitably suffer from mental illness or emotional disturbance, and that in fact the incidence of such disturbance is higher than in the general population. An example of the risks involved in placing a disturbed individual in a workshop environment was graphically put by one respondent: 'I was in the woodwork shop when a claw hammer was thrown as I walked from the work benches. [It was] thrown by a trainee prone to severe temper. The home environment aggravated the situation. I was hit in the back but suffered no injuries. The incident could have been serious.' To the outsider the incident may appear very serious, even if the outcome was not as disastrous as it could easily have been. One of the clearest examples of frustration leading to violence provided a rare touch of humour: 'Teams from two day centres had been playing netball, and the violence that arose was occasioned by the side that was losing.'

The fact that many staff working in ATCs considered violence towards themselves to be a common occurrence points to the need for closer examination of this area. The following incident was described as 'fairly typical' by a worker in a day centre where members took it in turn to serve tea: 'He became upset when he realised it was not his turn to serve and tried to lift a large table. When I and one other member of staff tried to restrain him he attacked me.' The study did not attempt to examine in detail every incident that involved staff in violence. Only the most recent example is described by respondents, and for this group in particular it was difficult to identify any common factors that precipitated violence.

Staff concern

Most of the day centre workers said that they were concerned by the threat of violence. The figure of 61 per cent was marginally higher than for fieldworkers (60 per cent) and for residential workers (56 per cent). Day centre workers were more concerned about the possibility of violence than about either publicity following inappropriate action or accountability for their actions. What may be surprising, however, is that they were the only group who expressed more concern over possible violence than over the issue of staffing levels in their centres. This is especially significant given the high representation of ATCs in the sample, and the general acknowledgement that staffing levels had not increased adequately to cope with their developing social and educational role. In other words, despite being asked to compare violence with a range of such pressing problems as publicity, accountability and staffing, day centre workers still regarded it as a greater source of concern.

The position changes, however, when we look at issues of pay and conditions of service, which day centre workers saw as being of greater concern than the possibility of violence. In comparison, the field workers and residential workers expressed no strong views one way or the other. Day centre workers had a similar response to residential workers over concern for their handling of a particular case, which they rated as more important than the possibility of violence. This point was picked up in a letter from a manager based at headquarters who expressed the view that 'staff are handicapped here by fear of damaging a relationship by calling the police and thus they put themselves at greater risk of violence'. This was not a negative criticism, but made in the context of an acknowledgement of the dilemma in which staff could be placed. Day care and residential staff may have as their primary aim the establishing of a positive, long term relationship with a client, and would regard the risk of violence as a price worth paying for its achievement. Calling in help might be seen as an admission of failure to achieve this primary aim. When we consider the questions of training and guidelines, we find that only one in five day care workers had received any guidance in the practical management of violence as part of their vocational training. 89 per cent considered it necessary to print guidelines concerned with the management of violence, and most thought that this should be the responsibility of the employer. There was unanimous affirmation that such guidelines should include advice on the legal position regarding physical restraint, and 92 per cent wanted advice on techniques of physical restraint.

Views on in-service training were also strong, with a full 100 per cent stating that training should include advice on the legal position regarding physical restraint, and 90 per cent wanting training to cover techniques of physical restraint. There are clear indications in Hampshire that such requests have become more vocal in the last couple of years, and the demand for guidelines and training materials has increased accordingly. The Solent branch of the SCA held a meeting on this subject, and Hampshire County Council Social Services Research Section is currently studying the level of violence in homes for elderly people.

A response to the Wessex study from a representative of the National Association of Teachers of the Mentally Handicapped (NATMH) indentified the following specific areas of concern for members:

(i)   lack of advice and training in prevention and management of violence on current training courses;
(ii) whether there was always the means to raise the alarm or call for assistance in an emergency;
(iii) whether staff knew what procedure should be adopted in a difficult situation;
(iv) the effect of staffing ratios on the incidence of violence;
(v)   whether staff knew the law relating to coping with violence;
(vi) lack of information given to staff about trainees;
(vii) whether staff knew the law relating to compensation for both physical injury and damage to property.

This list rather neatly summarises some of the main issues we have encountered repeatedly in this study, and some methods of meeting these concerns will be discussed in Chapter 8, on training.

The sample we have been able to consider has been limited in size and scope, and there is certainly room for a bigger study of violence towards day care staff. In the meantime, we have been able to indentify some common themes from the study, and the main conclusion must be that more attention should be given to violence in day care settings, and that priority should be accorded to the provision of training for staff.

Conclusions from the Wessex study

The Wessex study and our subsequent local interviews with staff suggest that the level of violence towards social workers is high enough to warrant serious discussions within agencies, followed by decisive action. For residential workers, parallels can be drawn and lessons learned from the problems of violence in hospitals over the past twenty years. The need for guidance and training has been strongly expressed by staff in the residential sector, and it needs to be offered more consistently in future. Proper acknowledgement of the problems and dilemmas faced by staff can reduce cynicism.

Conversely, if those outside the immediate residential home will not accept the reality of violence, or only offer bland guidelines and reassurances, then the alienation of staff will increase and more serious problems will be stored up for the future.

In examining violence towards fieldworkers, it was possible to identify a definite pattern. The involvement of workers in depriving children or mentally disordered people of liberty places them at far more risk than involvement in other aspects of their job. In future years, studies of violence towards approved social workers, probation officers, social workers responsible for children in care and so on might yield results that would help sort out the preventable from the unavoidable, and at least allow more discussion in an area that has been neglected.

American studies

For day care workers, we are somewhat limited in our ability to draw general conclusions from what was a small and biased sample. However, the need for training was clear. In contrast to the absence of detailed studies in the UK, there have been a number of studies in the USA where social work staff have been included in examinations of violence in community based centres. The main focus has been on community mental health centres. A theme emerges which, we believe, is being repeated in Britain, and that is that the shift from hospital or residential care to day hospital, day centres and community care has reached the point where some of the more violent patients are now more likely to be seen by a range of staff who will not always know details and patterns of the patient's history of violence. Additionally, in a day centre staff may not have sanctions such as segregation available whereas in a hospital, violence can be dealt with in a more self-contained way. Some of the American studies produce figures which make an interesting comparison with the Wessex study. One reported in 1976 covered 101 mental health workers in psychiatry, psychology and social work. 80 worked mainly with outpatients while the other 21 worked mainly with inpatients. Of the total group, 43 per cent had been threatened personally with violence over the previous year, while 24 per cent had actually been assaulted. The breakdown of actual violence victims by profession was as follows: 34 per cent of psychiatrists, 20 per cent of social workers, 7 per cent of psychologists (Whitman, 1976).

This fitted the picture drawn by Star, who noted three main points in a study of assaults on mental health workers.

(1) as a group, psychiatrists are most likely to be the targets of patient assaults and social workers the next most frequent target, (2) younger and less experienced clinicians of any discipline run a greater risk of being the victims of patient violence and (3) only a small percentage of clients, whether inpatients or outpatients physically assault mental health workers.

In another study reported by Bernstein (1981), respondents were involved in psychotherapy and included psychiatrists, psychologists, social workers and counsellors. Of the 422 respondents, 14 per cent reported actual physical assaults and 35 per cent said they had been threatened. In Bernstein's study, (as in any examination of violent incidents officially reported by staff), there was probably an underestimate of the number of incidents. Some staff believed that reporting an incident would be seen as an indication of poor work ability. Others saw violence as a part of the job which was to be expected and accepted, and they would therefore only report major incidents. Finally, some staff found completing a report an unnecessary chore.

Star (1984) considered that although underlying factors could be traced for many incidents (frustrations, provocation, the regime and so on), at the moment of crisis the violence often seemed totally unpredictable; also that social workers needed to be able to indentify certain danger signals in an interview:

● Fears or concerns expressed by the client about losing control, for example, the client may say, 'I'm going to blow my top', or may express vague fears of doing harm to someone.
● Evidence that the client has been looking for help, such as frequent calls to family or friends and appointments, kept or broken, with doctors or lawyers.

● Reports of action that suggest violence, such as purchasing a gun, driving recklessly, or throwing out all pills in the medicine cabinet (in case of an impulse to take an overdose).

Star also considered that, although signs of violence could sometimes be associated with angry brooding or sullen behaviour, it was more commonly signalled by a pattern of increased irritability, verbal outbursts, pacing up and down, restlessness, agitation or 'testing out' behaviour. We would conclude that staff in day centres may be particularly well placed to pick up some of these warning signals and convey them to colleagues. Encouraging the verbal expression of anger at this point might help the individual to keep control. The practitioner in Star was evident in some concluding comments:

> Simple sedation or restraint does not end the situation. Both the patient and the counsellor must deal with the aftermath. In a subsequent meeting with the client, discuss the violent episode openly and thoroughly and review the specific events which led to the loss of control . . . Following an assault, many counsellors feel uncomfortable about seeing violent clients again and tend to avoid or reduce contact with them.

Some of the American literature is very detailed in its advice. Edelman built on the commonly accepted view that everyone should have a clear idea of what their role should be in the event of violence occurring, with advice on a series of detailed steps to take if violence were seen as a possibility, including identifying which room to use for risky interviews and developing a code for communicating between staff (Edelman, 1978, pp. 460–2). Although this approach may seem excessive in most types of day centre, it may have validity in some, such as those dealing with potentially violent offenders or with disturbed people in crisis.

Conclusions

In one sense, day hospitals and day centres can be seen as taking over gradually from hospitals and residential institutions the role of being the places where most of the pressure is felt in trying to provide basic social services for people in need. Given the 'institutional violence' to which many day centre users have themselves been subjected (poor health, poor housing and so on), it is perhaps surprising that the level of physical violence is not even higher than that reported in the Wessex study. It is exceedingly hard for practitioners under personal attack to retain the wider perspective that enables them to contrast their experiences with the forms of institutional violence detailed by Liazos (1977). Where the level of violence is particularly high, staff must strive to avoid slipping into a state of mind that attributes the cause of the violence directly to the personal characteristics of the users.

2

Understanding Violence

The purpose of this chapter is to explore some of the ideas that underlie our popular understanding of violence, and more specifically to consider those theories which may have practical value in reducing and controlling violent behaviour. The relevant literature is extensive, and much of it emanates from the United States, reflecting the very real preoccupations of academic research in a society possessing about 135 million guns and experiencing approximately 12 500 murders by gunfire each year. This literature is concerned with the psychology of *aggression*, and before proceeding further it is important to clarify our usage of the words 'violence' and 'aggression'.

'Violence' may usefully be defined as destructive behaviour, including physical assault, that is intended to injure a creature's own kind. In law, violence is 'the unlawful exercise of force'; more commonly, it is regarded as the deliberate infliction of physical injury on another, or the threat of doing such harm. The term 'aggression' has much broader meaning; it may be defined as an attacking process, by which dominance is gained. In the psychoanalytic tradition it has been seen as an instinct associated with hate and destructiveness, whereas in the Europe of the 1930s aggression meant simply 'unprovoked attack'. Students of animal behaviour, such as Konrad Lorenz, regard aggression as 'the fighting instinct in beast and man which is directed *against* members of the same species' (1966, p. ix). Anthony Storr, writing in the psychoanalytic tradition (1968), stresses the positive functions of aggression in spacing the population, selecting a mate, defending the young and creating order. In this chapter we are simply concerned with the usefulness of various theories of aggression in understanding violence. Mainly, we are considering one of two kinds of violence, 'expressive' violence, as opposed to 'instrumental' violence. Expressive violence gives vent to feelings of rage, often in reaction to provocation or frustration. In contrast, instrumental violence is committed for a rational motive, as the means to an end, and is commonly termed 'cold-blooded'. Although social work staff, like France in 1940, might conceivably become the victims of instrumental violence, the research described in the last chapter suggests that they are much more likely to become involved in 'red-blooded', expressive violence, which is the main concern of this book.

The literature of aggression is enlivened by fierce conflict between those whom Ashley Montagu (1978) calls the 'Innate Aggressionists', and the 'Social Learning' theorists. It is beyond the scope of this book to attempt to resolve this particular debate, and instead we shall consider the usefulness of what each has to offer. The 'Innate Aggressionists' comprise a diverse group, including Freud, Konrad Lorenz, Robert Ardrey, Desmond Morris and Anthony Storr, among others; they share the notion that aggression is both inborn and universal in human beings. The 'Social Learning' theorists draw on the work of behavioural psychologists to support the contention that aggressive behaviour is learned rather than innate. The first group has had enormous influence on popular conceptions of violence, through such books as Lorenz's 'On Aggression' (1966), Ardrey's 'The Territorial Imperative' (1966), Morris's 'The Naked Ape' (1967) and Storr's 'Human Aggression' (1968). Social workers merely reflect a widespread acceptance of these ideas when they discuss the provision of activity groups as 'outlets' for the aggressive drives of their young delinquent clients. The second group, the 'Social Learning' theorists, are less familiar, but their notion that violence is learned has interesting implications for its reduction. In between these two groups we shall also consider physiological factors in aggression, and the hypothesis that frustration causes violence.

Aggression as an instinct

The belief that violence is inborn can be traced back through nineteenth-century notions of man's 'Innate Depravity' and the pessimistic seventeenth-century philosophy of Thomas Hobbes, to early Christian doctrines of original sin and Old Testament commandments against manslaughter. For our purposes, it will suffice to begin with Freud, who came late to the idea of a 'death instinct' as he reflected upon the massacres of the First World War. In 'Reflections on War and Death' he wrote that 'the very emphasis of the Commandment: Thou shalt not kill, makes it certain that we are descended from an endlessly long chain of generations of murderers whose love of murder was in their blood as it is perhaps also in our own' (1918, p. 60).

In 1920, 'Beyond the Pleasure Principle' advanced the notion of 'thanotos', an instinct which leads living beings towards death, in contrast with the sexual instinct, which constantly seeks renewal of life. The concept of a death instinct, unlike the idea of libido, did not become widely accepted among psychoanalysts. It is important because it represents an early attempt to understand the psychology of aggression, and because Freud went on to explore the idea that aggression is a projection of the individual's innate, self-destructive instinct. In 'Civilisation and its Discontents', he claimed that 'a powerful measure of desire for aggression has to be reckoned as part of man's instinctual endowment' and that 'the tendency to aggression is an innate, independent, instinctual disposition in man' (1930, p. 102). Freud saw the inwardly-directed death instinct as dangerous to the individual, and considered that it could be made less dangerous either by 'erotizing' it – combining it with libido in the form of sadism or masochism – or by directing it outwards in the form of aggression against others (Brown, 1961, p. 27).

Behaving aggressively towards other people is the simplest and most obvious way of providing an outlet for aggression, but Freudian theory also suggests two other potential outlets. One of these is *displacement*, a process in which aggressive energy is redirected towards a substitute person or object. The other is *sublimation*, a process in which instinctual energies are rechannelled towards constructive and creative activities. Both concepts have become popular, unlike the 'death instinct'. Of the two, displacement is more relevant to our theme. One wonders how many of the victims of assaults on staff reported earlier in this book were the recipients of violence that did not 'belong' to them, aggression that was displaced and redirected towards the nearest convenient target figure.

Konrad Lorenz approaches the subject of aggression from the standpoint of ethology, the science of animal behaviour. He observes that aggressive behaviour is widespread in the natural world, but that most animals stop short at killing their own kind. Unlike Freud, Lorenz rejects the idea of a 'death instinct', and instead he emphasises the functions of aggression in preserving the species. Three functions are identified in the world of vertebrate animals. Firstly, males fight for the best females, so that the characteristics of the victor are transmitted to the next generation in a process that Charles Darwin called natural selection. Secondly, animals fight to establish and defend sufficient territory to meet their needs for food. Thirdly, many creatures struggle to establish hierarchies of dominance, a carefully defined ranking order in which each animal knows its place and which helps to maintain a stable social order. (The study of dominance hierarchies dates back to 1913, when a Danish scientist, Thorleif Schjelderup-Ebbe, noticed and described the fact that each hen in his coop could peck any hen below it in the hierarchy, but was in turn liable to be pecked by any hen above it.)

Lorenz regards the aggressive drive in both animals and man as an instinct, rather than a reaction to external circumstances. The popular and influential books of another student of animal behaviour, Desmond Morris, have much in common with Lorenz. But while Lorenz maintains that aggressive behaviour arises spontaneously, Morris sees it as a genetically determined response to various environmental conditions, and to signals transmitted by others. *Manwatching – a Field Guide to Human Behaviour* (1978) is a profusely illustrated and fascinating presentation of Morris's ideas, deserving of attention by anyone engaged in social work. For instance, a section on 'Submissive Behaviour' (p. 142) illustrates Morris's belief that aggression can be controlled by innate appeasement gestures. Photographs of people bowing, prostrating themselves and otherwise making themselves smaller reminded us of an incident described to us recently by a young female worker in a probation hostel. When she was threatened by a male resident wielding a knife, she 'instinctively' sat on the floor. This impulsive appeasement behaviour had the immediate effect of reducing the man's aggression; he calmed down, and the incident ended peacefully.

Stanley Kubrick's classic science fiction film *2001 – A Space Odyssey* opens with a vivid and arresting scene in which man's primitive ancestors first discover how to use bones as weapons in hunting animals for food, and then, in defence of their territory, go on to smash the heads of their fellow creatures. This sequence provides a perfect illustration of the ideas of Robert Ardrey, whose books *African Genesis* (1961) and *The Territorial Imperative* (1966) have shared the popularity of Lorenz and Morris. Ardrey shares with Lorenz the belief that aggression is instinctual, and closely linked with territoriality. His ideas start from the notion that primitive man's use of weapons led him to an upright stance, the development of the thumb, and eventually the enlargement of the brain. In Ardrey's own words, 'Far from the truth lay the antique assumption that man had fathered the weapon. The weapon, instead, had fathered man. The mightiest of predators had come about as the logical conclusion to an evolutionary transition.' It is important to note that Ardrey approaches aggression from the standpoint of a writer and dramatist; his ideas are challenged by many scientists.

The final 'innate aggressionist' to be mentioned here is Anthony Storr, who brings together the seminal ideas of Freud, the more recent theories of Ardrey and Lorenz, and a number of other authors. Storr's book *Human Aggression* concludes that 'aggression is a drive as innate, as natural, and as powerful as sex . . . the theory that aggression is nothing but a response to frustration is no longer tenable . . . the aggressive drive is an inherited constant . . . and is absolutely necessary for survival' (1968, p. 148). This conclusion is preceded by a useful series of chapters on aggression at various stages of human development, between the sexes, and in relation to a range of psychiatric disorders. Again, this book has particular value for social workers; for instance, Storr states that 'aggression in the female is only fully aroused in response to threat, especially if the young are involved' (p. 86). The previous chapter's example of a situation where care proceedings were in hand provides vivid support for this view: 'Mother coldly stated she'd probably kill me.'

Another illustration of Storr's relevance is to be found in his treatment of schizoid aggression, a subject in which, in our experience, social workers are prone to make wild generalisations. Storr reminds us that 'the disposal of aggression is particularly difficult for schizoid people . . . when rebuff or criticism, however mild, are interpreted as insult, withdrawal or murder may seem the only possible alternative' (p. 120).

The ideas of the innate aggressionists, through the books mentioned above, films like *2001* and novels like William Golding's *Lord of the Flies* have been so pervasive in our everyday understanding of aggression that the counter-arguments of their critics seem to have gone by default, as far as popular culture is concerned. And yet there is a substantial academic literature which questions some of the assumptions of the 'innate' school, sets out the contrasting ideas of social learning theory, and also has much to offer the social worker confronted by the violent client. A useful and representative selection of this literature is to be found in *Man and Aggression* (2nd edition, 1973), a collection of essays edited by Ashley Montagu. The varied and diverse contributions are linked by their common contention that human behaviour is learned. Montagu's own view is simply stated: 'We know that by far the larger proportion of child-batterers were themselves battered or neglected as children. We know that those who have been emotionally deprived are likely to turn into aggressive adults. And we also know that those who have been adequately loved as children are likely to develop into loving, unaggressive adults' (1978, p. 7). The emphasis here is upon knowledge based upon empirical evidence, rather than theory, which is concerned with the interpretation of that evidence.

One of the essayists in Montagu's collection, John Hurrell Crook, reminds us of a study once widely used in social work training, 'Patterns of Child Rearing' (1957), by Sears, Maccoby and Levin. Their work demonstrated that aggressive children are likely to come from homes where aggressive behaviour is heavily punished, and where there is an absence of family rules. But by the age of twelve, such children show less aggression than those from permissive homes where there is an absence of punishment as well as of rules. The least aggressive children came from homes where strong rules proscribed aggressive behaviour, which was controlled by non-punitive methods, including the withdrawal of affection. This kind of child-rearing seemed to produce children with strong consciences.

These findings are not incompatible with the concept of an aggressive instinct, although they stress learning. Interestingly Anthony Storr, whose ideas are criticised elsewhere in Montagu's collection, provides us with some near-perfect anecdotal illustrations of social learning theory from an habitual criminal:

> Violence is in a way like bad language – something that a person like me's been brought up with, something I got used to very early on as part of the daily scene of childhood, you might say. I don't at all recoil from the idea, I don't have a sort of inborn dislike of the thing, like you do. As long as I can remember I've seen violence in use all around me – my mother hitting the children; my brothers and sister all whacking our mother, or other children; the man downstairs bashing his wife and so on.

and

> . . . the only way we knew to answer violence was with violence back again. That was always axiomatic. If somebody sloshed you, you sloshed him; if you weren't big enough, you got somebody else to do it for you. It was as much a part of everyday life and behaviour as the houses, was violence. (Parker and Allerton, 1962, pp. 93 and 36)

Many of the essays in Montagu's collection contain refutations of the ideas of Lorenz and Ardrey too detailed for summary here: but the general flavour is conveyed by J. P. Scott's assertion that 'all stimulation of aggression eventually comes from forces present in the environment' (Montagu, 1973, p. 154). Scott reminds us that 'fighting is a complex phenomenon, taking many forms, and is stimulated and controlled by many different factors. Any "single factor" explanation, such as that of instinct, is necessarily incomplete'

(p. 140). And John Hurrell Crook concludes his particularly thorough contribution with the statement that 'aggressive behaviour occurs normally as a response to particular aversive stimuli and ceases upon their removal. The prevalence of aggression in modern man may thus be attributed to aversive features in the complex, overcrowded, overcompetitive, over-stratified social world in which he lives rather than to some unsatisfied vital urge' (p. 214).

Physiological factors

Before exploring some of the ideas of social learning theory, it is important to remind ourselves of physiological factors in aggressive behaviour. The study of physiological factors, like the concept of man's innate depravity, has a long history. The nineteenth-century Italian psychiatrist Cesare Lombroso, influenced by the new thinking of Charles Darwin, compared the skull shapes and measurements of criminals and non-criminals, and suggested that persistent criminals were atavistic 'throw-backs' to some previous stage of human evolution. The development of statistical methods later contradicted his theory, but elements of Lombrosian thinking have lingered on. Lombroso found his criminals in Italian gaols, and British gaols provided the human material for criminological research in the 1960s that concerned itself with chromosome abnormalities in males. Normal males have a pair of chromosomes in each body cell associated with 'sex-linked' characteristics, one of which is described as an 'X' chromosome, the other as a 'Y' chromosome. In rare individuals, the usual 'XY' pairing is missing, and unusual combinations such as 'XYY' and 'XXY' are found instead. These abnormalities have been associated with low intelligence and mental subnormality, and the 'XYY' syndrome has been linked with unusual aggressiveness. Males with the 'XYY' pattern are fifteen times more common in prisons than in the general population. But the mass media stereotype of the 'XYY' male as an uncontrollably aggressive psychopath is quite misleading. Such men tend to be excessively tall and of low intelligence, and this combination may make them particularly liable to criminal prosecution; moreover, many 'XYY' prisoners have been convicted of property offences, rather than violence. Lefkowitz *et al.* point out that 'before we can conclude that this extra Y chromosome is a genetic precursor to aggressive behaviour, more . . . data are required' (1977, p. 17). So the research in this field remains inconclusive.

The extensive literature concerned with the *psychology* of aggression is complemented by a similarly extensive literature concerned with its *physiology*. In 1915 W. B. Cannon published *Bodily Changes in Pain, Hunger, Fear and Rage*. His observations remain valid and significant, and are well summarised by Anthony Storr:

> When anger is aroused in mammals, there is an increase in pulse rate and blood pressure, together with an increase in the peripheral circulation of the blood, and a rise in the level of blood glucose. The rate of breathing is accelerated, and the muscles of the limbs and trunk become more tensely contracted and less liable to fatigue . . . blood is diverted from the internal organs of the body, and digestion and the movements of the intestine cease, although the flow of acid and the digestive juice tends to be increased. In animals, and possibly also in man, the hair stands on end; and the picture of rage is completed by baring the teeth and the emission of involuntary noises. During anger, there is also a diminution of sensory perception. (1968, p. 28)

Although there are obvious dangers in applying analogies from the animal world directly to human beings, this description of the arousal state that may precede fight or flight will not be entirely unfamiliar to social work staff whose clients have either attacked them or fled from the scene.

More recent work in this field has focused upon the complex functions of the brain and related hormonal systems, using surgery and electrical stimulation on experimental animals. There is general agreement that a small part of the lower brain, the hypothalamus, is associated with several emotions, and in particular the pattern of 'rage' described by Cannon, which it appears to control. Normally, the hypothalamus is itself controlled by the cerebral cortex (the 'higher brain'), and the expression of anger is inhibited. However, when some sudden external threat appears, the cerebral cortex appears to release its normal control of the hypothalamus, which in turn releases various hormones that produce a state of angry arousal. This arousal state may persist for some time after the threat has disappeared, an important point for social work staff to note. This arousal state itself may produce angry feelings, in a circular, self-reinforcing process. The role of hormones in this process is confirmed by various experiments, including one in which the male sex hormone testosterone was given to animals, with the result that their threshold for aggressive response was lowered (Montagu, 1973, p. 195). Anthony Storr concludes that 'the body contains a co-ordinated physico-chemical system which subserves the emotions and actions which we call aggressive, and that this system is easily brought into action both by the stimulus of threat, and also by frustration' (1968, p. 30). The existence of this system is not disputed. The point to notice is the need for some external stimulus or threat to activate the system. As the biologist J. P. Scott puts its, 'there is no need for fighting . . . there is no such thing as a simple "instinct for fighting" in the sense of an internal driving force which has to be satisfied' (Bailey, 1977, p. 30).

Frustration and aggression

The word 'frustration' has been mentioned more than once in this chapter, and 'frustration' is perhaps the shortest and simplest possible answer to the question 'What causes violence?' But behind that deceptively obvious assertion lie 40 years of controversy and ingenious psychological experiments. 'Frustration' is generally defined as the outcome of interference with a person's progress towards a goal that he desires, and it is clearly an emotion that affects social work practice all the time. It is equally true that there are many occasions on which the reduction of a person's frustrated feelings can reduce dramatically the likelihood of his becoming violent. But this does not mean that frustration necessarily causes violence. Violence is more likely when a person close to a goal is blocked in his progress than when the goal is distant. In one experiment, psychologists deliberately broke into supermarket checkout queues. The strongest aggressive reactions came from shoppers near the front of the queue, and close to their goal; shoppers who had just joined the queue did not seem so upset (Bailey, 1977, p. 93).

There are two major weaknesses in the notion that frustration causes violence. The first is that aggressive behaviour often occurs without the aggressor experiencing any frustrated feelings beforehand. The second is that frustration can produce a number of different reactions, of which violence is only one. Others include restlessness, tension, destructiveness, apathy, fantasy, regression, and the adoption of repetitive, fixated behaviour. Nevertheless, frustration is so commonly present in social work encounters that staff should always be sensitive to the possibility that it may lead their clients into a violent outburst.

Aggression as learned behaviour

So far, we have briefly considered a range of ideas that have undoubtedly shaped and influenced our understanding of human aggression, living as we do in an era which has witnessed mass violence on a scale unprecedented in history. Freud, Lorenz, Morris and Storr, despite their differences of emphasis, share the belief that human beings are born with an innate aggressive drive, an instinct which must be satisfied and given outlet, controlled, sublimated or rechannelled into some constructive activity. We have also seen how the human body contains a co-ordinated arousal system, which would seem to support the idea that aggression is innate. But we have noted that this system is generally activated by some external factor, such as a sudden threat or intolerable frustration. We have in addition noticed how violent behaviour may be learned in childhood as acceptable and normal in some situations. A twin stress on the external causes of aggression and the learning of aggressive behaviour distinguishes the 'social learning' theorists from the 'innate aggressionists', and it is to these theories that we now turn. The implications of the idea that humans are innately violent are rather gloomy; all we can do with a powerful instinct is to try to control it. The implications of social learning theory are correspondingly optimistic; we can learn new responses to threatening situations, and we can do a great deal to change the immediate enviroment and modify particular situations.

The starting point of learning theory is stated succinctly by Kenneth Boulding; man's genes endow him with 'an enormous nervous system of some 10 billion components, the informational content of which is derived almost wholly from the environment, that is, from inputs into the organism from outside. The genetic contribution to man's nervous system is virtually complete at birth. Almost everything that happens thereafter is learned' (Montagu, 1973, pp. 171–2). This statement neatly complements our two earlier quotations describing a violent childhood, and leads us into the ideas of Albert Bandura, who has developed a model of aggression based on learning theory (1973a and 1973b). His model has three main elements: the origins of aggressive behaviour, the factors which instigate or provoke it, and the factors which reinforce and maintain it. Bandura maintains that most behaviour, including aggressive behaviour, is acquired through observation and imitation. This happens firstly within the family, then within a particular subculture, and thirdly through modelling behaviour depicted by the mass media, especially television. Western culture provides its children with a continuous stream of opportunites to observe and learn about violence; it is estimated that by the age of eighteen, the average young American will have seen 18 000 murders on television, and similar findings have been made in other Western countries. A very substantial body of research literature indicates that children who have witnessed violence are more likely to behave aggressively afterwards, and that they become progressively more insensitive to the suffering of others (Bailey, 1977, pp. 60–8; Belson, 1978). It may also be the case that the depiction of real violence in news broadcasts has more profound effects than the portrayal of fictional violence.

The second element in Bandura's theory of aggression concerns those factors which activate and provoke violent behaviour. He lists five groups of factors, the first of which involves seeing other people acting violently. This may not only arouse an onlooker who has previously learned how to be violent; it can also suggest that violence is acceptable, even worthy of approval, in some situations. This process can sometimes be observed at football matches, for example. The second group of factors includes threats, insults, direct assault and simple frustration. The third group covers situations in which an individual expects to gain something from acting aggressively. The fourth group comprises situations in which people are ordered to be violent by someone in authority, having previously been trained to do so. The fifth and last group of instigators is largely concerned with people suffering from psychotic conditions who may, for example, be impelled by inner voices to harm others.

The third main element of Bandura's theory examines how aggressive behaviour is reinforced. Reinforcement happens in many different ways. Acting violently may bring status within one's peer group. Responding aggressively may turn out to be an effective way of meeting insult or attack. Some people become more violent when their victim shows signs of pain and suffering, although other aggressors may be inhibited by an injured victim; the evidence on this question is inconclusive. Aggressive behaviour and fighting prowess may become a source of pride and self-esteem for those whose early socialisation did not train them to feel guilty about it. Such individuals may find it easier to regard their victims as less than human.

Violent incidents

Bandura's theory of aggression lays great stress on those factors in aggressive behaviour that are external to the individual, and located within his family, his subculture and his total environment. In the remaining part of this chapter we shall look more closely at the specific situations in which a violent incident may occur, and at the practical implications of this approach.

Social psychologists suggest that there are four ingredients present in the majority of violent incidents (Bailey, 1977, p. 83); these ingredients are

    I – A state of arousal
    II – A trigger
    III – A weapon
    IV – A target,

and we shall consider each in turn.

With very few exceptions, human beings are unable to behave aggressively unless they are aroused. Arousal is both a mental and a physical state; as we have noted, it involves a faster heartbeat and accelerated breathing, and may also include shaking or clammy hands and a flushed face. Recent research suggests that any kind of excitement can produce the same general state of arousal, which may find expression in the form of fear, joy or sexual desire, as well as anger and aggression. One kind of emotion may rapidly be replaced by another in the aroused person; erotic arousal, for instance, may easily be transformed into a violent quarrel between lovers. In one experiment, students who had watched an erotic film were even more willing to administer electric shocks to others than students who had watched a violent film (Bailey, 1977, p. 85). This close association between different forms of arousal may be linked with the fact that the hypothalamus is very close to other parts of the brain that produce strong emotion.

A state of arousal may be produced by many different causes. Frustration, which we have already considered, is one. Another is simple physical pain. Hot and humid weather seems to be associated with violent urban riots. Aggressive threats can evoke angry arousal in the threatened person, and a hostile stare can have the same effect. Invading someone's 'personal space' by getting too close to them is frequently seen as aggressive, arousing behaviour.

The second ingredient in most violent incidents is some kind of 'trigger'. In this context, a trigger is defined as an event which releases a state of arousal and transforms it into an angry outburst. The trigger event may be some trivial remark or gesture, and may be quite unrelated to the frustration, pain or threat that produced arousal. The presence of a weapon or a target may act as a trigger. Anything which serves to heighten an existing state of arousal may precipitate actual violence.

The third necessary ingredient is a weapon. In the absence of suitable objects, the fist and the booted foot can cause plenty of damage. But the use of seemingly innocuous objects can greatly increase the range and potential damage of violent behaviour. Heavy ashtrays, chairs and even a sewing machine have been thrown at social work staff. Knives are obvious weapons, including such variations as paper knives and sharpened steel combs, and all sharp objects have lethal potential. Guns are fortunately rarely encountered by social workers in Britain; their effects have been widely studied in the United States, because of their special ability to distance the aggressor from the effects of his violence. Motor vehicles, on the other hand, are part of our society; although they may not be regarded as weapons, they offer frightening possibilities for the expression of aggressive feelings.

The fourth and final ingredient is a target. The sex, social status and behaviour of a potential victim will affect an aggressor in various ways. Traditionally brought up middle class males may be inhibited against assaulting women, for example, and there may also be inhibitions against attacking someone who is perceived as having greater social status than oneself. The behaviour of the victim may be consciously or unconsciously provocative. Sally Green, a Southampton social worker who was beaten around the head and shoulders by a female client at the end of a home visit, has described to us how she *walked* back to her car while she was repeatedly struck. With hindsight, she feels that she would have been less hurt had she run, but at the time, she felt that to have fled would have involved her in additional surrender and loss of self-respect (Green, 1982).

We have already noted that social work staff may become the victims of violence that does not 'belong' to them, and it is important to remember that the target of aggression may have nothing to do with its instigation. Freud's concept of displacement has direct, practical relevance to situations in which the 'proper' target is elusive or absent, and another person may unwittingly be available as a target for displaced fury.

Implications for practice

The four-stage model that has just been outlined is simple to describe, and perhaps it labours the obvious. But this should make it all the easier to remember in situations of stress and tension, when the removal or absence of any single ingredient – arousal, trigger, weapon or target – may prevent a violent incident. 'Prevention' is a theme of this book, but in stressing it we recognise that many of the incidents that affect social work staff are unpredictable. The attack on Sally Green is an example of an assault that could not have been foreseen. The most expert prediction of risk has only a roughly even chance of success. A discussion of the difficulties of prediction techniques may be found in Floud and Young (1983).

Conclusion

In this chapter, we have briefly mentioned a wide range of theories about the causes of aggressive behaviour. Their respective protagonists sometimes give the impression that if they are right, the others must be wrong; if, for example, one accepts that aggression is an inborn instinct, then the contributions of learning theory may safely be ignored. On the other hand, Leonard Berkowitz claims that 'our behaviour is influenced by our experiences *and* our inherited biological characteristics' (Montagu, 1973, p. 40). We have presented various ideas in the belief that all of them have value in increasing our understanding of violence. In our view, there is no reason why a particular incident of aggressive behaviour should not be examined from a variety of different standpoints, each of which may have practical implications for its handling. We have just noted, for instance, the relevance of the long-established psychoanalytic concept of 'displacement' to a more modern approach that analyses violent situations.

Broadly speaking, the two main groups of ideas that we have considered, the 'innate aggressionists' and the 'social learning' theorists, have corresponding implications for the reduction of violence. If human beings accumulate 'aggressive tension' over time, then there is a need to provide outlets for its periodic discharge. If violence is simply a response to aggressive stimuli in the environment, then the need is to alter our surrounding conditions. There is no reason why we should not attempt to do both. There is much evidence to support the value of hard physical work, creative effort, and playing in aggressive sports. Such activities often make people feel better afterwards; however, they do not necessarily make us feel more peaceable. Physical activity may itself be arousing, and aggressive behaviour on a sports field may be imitated by others. So to provide outlets for aggression may not, on its own, be enough.

The implication of the idea that aggressive behaviour is learned is that non-violent behaviour can also be learned. The implications of the idea that violent incidents usually involve arousal, a trigger, a weapon and target are that an aroused person should be given time (at least 20 minutes) to cool off, that inadvertent triggers, both words and actions, should be avoided, that potential weapons should not be lying around, and that people who are potential targets should behave carefully so as not to provoke or unwittingly incite violence. All this may be obvious in theory and not so simple in practice. But there is great value in talking calmly, listening sensitively and adopting postures that do not threaten someone who is aroused. In the following chapters we shall look more closely at recognising potential violence, preventing it whenever possible, and responding appropriately when actual violence occurs.

3
Recognising Potential Violence

Throughout this book we shall, as far as is possible, be stressing the need to prevent violent incidents arising in the first instance. Secondly, we shall look at the need to ensure that if violence does occur it is handled professionally and competently so that the least amount of trauma is caused. The objective of this chapter is, therefore, to try to identify some of the circumstances in which violence might occur, as well as to consider some of the medical features of people who appear to be predisposed to violence.

It will sometimes be necessary for practitioners and managers to discuss and decide what action should be taken when a set of circumstances or individual potential for violence has been identified. Apart from preparing for the immediate future, some will want to consider annotating records in such a way as to warn other staff members who might become involved later. Others may feel this would be unnecessary or would even constitute an infringement of civil liberties. Inevitably, there will be some occasions when violence arises for no obvious reason, and illustrations of this will be provided to demonstrate that sometimes there is no way in which it can be avoided.

Measuring violence

From an ethological perspective, we have already noted the relationship between violence and aggression. Animals often maintain order within their group by exhibiting a potential for aggression rather than by being aggressive. Similarly, human beings often show aggressive signs without hurting each other. We refer to 'tackling a problem' or 'fighting against adversity' and, in this way, intellectual or social achievement is sometimes gained. Whilst this sort of aggression is necessary to life, violence is not. Aggression is often a positive force for good; violence, on the other hand is usually negative and destructive. Nevertheless, not all violence can be easily condemned as unnecessary or without good reason. A soldier at war might by very violent in disposing of enemy troops and, for such, could be considered a hero. On the other hand the actions of a soldier who uses violence to beat up a prisoner of war would be strongly condemned. Value judgements will depend, therefore, upon the intention and motivation of the violent person, and whether the violence is coldly calculated (instrumental) or impulsive and uncontrolled (expressive).

Statistics in respect of violent acts must be interpreted with some caution; what is considered 'violent' depends very much upon our threshold view, a point made very clearly by Belson (1978) in his research into television violence and the adolescent boy. Belson decided that a special measuring system was needed in order to determine the size of the violence problem. He started with a broad definition by describing it as behaviour of a kind that produced or was likely to produce hurt or harm of any kind to the object on the receiving end. This object could be animate or inanimate and the hurt or harm could be psychological or physical. He investigated such behaviour within a six month period of the lifetime of 1565 London boys aged 12 to 17 years, using a complex measuring technique which eventually enabled him to categorise each act on an illustrated grading scale, namely: 'only very slightly violent', 'a bit violent', 'fairly violent', 'quite violent', 'very violent', 'extremely violent'. Each of these six categories was illustrated with a list of acts of violence with the intention of helping raters classify the various acts of violence of each boy.

This set of illustrations had been empirically developed through the ratings of the public . . . we had gone to the public after clear evidence of major disagreement amongst our rating staff about where on the scale of seriousness different acts should be put. It was thought that an illustrated scale would anchor the system against major disagreements and that since the public had in fact been a principal source of the hypotheses being investigated, they should be used in developing the illustrations.

However, there was early evidence once this operation was started of sharp discord amongst the public, too, about how different acts should be rated. In the end, we settled for illustrative acts about which the public tended less to disagree and the rating of the thousands of acts of violence derived from boys was carried out against such illustrations. The issue of disagreement is worthy of note in its own right, for it suggests an underlying lack of consensus in our society about the seriousness of different acts of violence and in all likelihood of greater permissiveness about violent behaviour on the part of some people than on the part of others.

In some cultures, violence can be synonymous with affection and the victim will only become concerned when the beating stops because that could indicate a certain amount of indifference. This is important in the context of recognising potential violence because an understanding of cultural norms will sometimes provide useful pointers as well as an indication of the threshold limits of what is acceptable.

In a recorded case of Non-Accidental Injury to a 10 year old boy in Hampshire, his 31 year old brother (who was also his legal guardian) admitted beating the boy with a telephone cable because it was something his own father would have done. To prove the point, the guardian was able to display scars of wounds which had been inflicted by his father several years ago.

In an examination of parents who had neglected or battered their children, Dr Susan Isaacs (1972) found that as children they had often suffered from parental neglect or battering themselves. It seems that violence to children often occurred when parents experienced stress, resulting from frustration and the need to be seen as good parents. This is not a book about violence in families, but it may be a fair assumption that compared with the general population, parents who inflict severe physical punishment upon their children would more readily give vent to their negative feelings and emotions towards professionals. However, we are not aware of any research on this subject. Weller (1984) is of the view that 'A child who has serious difficulties with his parents will necessarily be disturbed, and the father's violence towards the mother was found to be the most important contributing factor in a study of 21 homicidally aggressive children.'

Are there common factors which help to identify abusing parents and, therefore, assist us when trying to identify potential staff abusers? Attempts have been made to devise comprehensive systems to categorise child abuse and neglect (Oates, 1979), but most of the professionals involved in working with relatives of abused children would probably agree with Doyle and Oates (1980) that every person and every family is unique and occasionally a family will fit into no particular classification. Nevertheless, '. . . certain factors run through all groups, most notably isolation, stress and violent experiences in a parent's own childhood. Alcohol and certain drugs act as disinhibiting factors which may contribute to abuse in all groups.'

These are some of the factors that social work staff need to be aware of in order to recognise potential violence.

Situational violence

Situational violence can sometimes be predicted and anticipated even when there is nothing specific in the history of the case which suggests a violent outcome. The deprivation of liberty is likely to be a common denominator and could arise when Place of Safety Orders are being served or when formal admissions are being attempted under the Mental Health legislation (see Chapter 1). In February 1985, Peter Durrant, a social worker experienced with mentally ill people, was trying to escort a patient to psychiatric hospital in a car driven by a police officer. The car crashed and the patient died; Peter Durrant sustained serious injuries. To a much lesser extent, the provision of care under Section 47 of the National Assistance Act sometimes produces violent reactions from old people who do not wish to be uprooted from their own homes.

Medical conditions

We know of no conclusive scientific evidence to substantiate claims that are sometimes made that violence in psychiatric hospitals is increasing, or that people suffering from mental illness are particularly prone to violent behaviour. If anything, it would seem from Fottrell's research study (1980), which looked at the incidence of violence in three large mental hospitals, that there was little violence and that which did occur tended to be of a minor nature. Weller (1984) makes the interesting observation, however, that

Since 1954 the number of patients in Mental hospitals, in England and Wales has declined by 67 000, but only 3010 ex patients are supported by local authorities . . . as a society we have been failing in our care of schizophrenics. Their difficulties in obtaining psychiatric treatment, their high suicide rates after discharge from hospital, and the prevalence of serious mental illness among the destitute and in prison, are further indictments of 'Community Care' policies.

Weller concludes that there is a direct link between violence in our society and the neglect of mental illness by successive governments. There are a number of medical conditions which sometimes lead to aggressive or violent behaviour. According to Weller (1984) 'Hallucinations, delusions, and conceptual disorganisation create obvious hazards and psychotic manifestations of this kind – particularly when associated with thought disorder – have been shown to predict violence on an acute admission ward.' Research carried out by Taylor and Gunn (1984) included an analysis of the records of 1241 men who had been remanded in Brixton prison and showed that in the group charged with homicide just over a third were psychiatrically abnormal; five (11 per cent) of those convicted were schizophrenic.

What sort of people are prone to violence? Some support has been found for Megargee's view that they are distributed biomodally; at one end of the curve are the over controlled, highly provoked individuals who eventually react with homicide rather than abuse or lesser violence, whilst at the other end – more commonly – are the under controlled, explosive psychopaths.

The temperamental component in some violent behaviour may be recognised early in childhood. Recurrent problems with feeding, bathing and dressing, together with loud crying, protest at novelty and tantrums are all more common in children who are later found to have 'conduct disorders', and such a history is general in adult criminals. (Weller, 1984)

Williams (1978), taking a less scientific approach, includes acute organic or functional psychosis, toxic confusional states, schizophrenia, manic excitement and hysteria in a summary of medical conditions where violent tendencies might be present. In the next chapter we shall also consider physiological factors which should be taken into account when people suffer from biochemical disorders such as Diabetes Mellitus.

Effect of drugs and alcohol

In all the illnesses listed above, the effects of drugs and alcohol, taken together or separately, are likely to influence seriously the behaviour pattern. This is equally so for people suffering from personality disorders.

Alcohol is responsible for many episodes of actual or threatened violence, but evidence that a patient has been drinking does not, of course, preclude other possible causes for his behaviour. The most common manifestation in the casualty department is the demanding and obstreperous drunk who is too agitated to sleep and too lacking in judgment to keep quiet. He makes everyone angry, but is usually relatively docile when confronted by experienced nursing staff and uniformed police. Sometimes, however, the disinhibiting effect of alcohol releases verbal abuse and aggressive postures which are but the prelude to actual violence. Rarely, but more dangerously, alcoholic intoxication can precipitate an acute paranoid state characterized by irrational, combative and destructive behaviour. (Williams, 1978, p. 36)

The Criminal Injuries Compensation Board has indicted that a significant number of their applicants have been victims of assault in which the consumption of alcohol played a significant part (CICB, 1983). There is no doubt that excessive alcohol intake leads to disinhibition which, in turn, sometimes produces violent incidents. This was acknowledged by the

Department of Health and Social Security when it provided the following notes of guidance for health authorities.

> Violence may be associated with the use or misuse of drugs, or alcohol (or both) or other toxic substances. Such patients may not always see themselves as ill and may feel threatened by, and react against, the alien environment in which they find themselves. In alcoholism treatment units acts of violence are uncommon: alcoholics are more likely to create a problem in a medical or surgical ward or in the accident or emergency department, very occasionally by violence in the true sense, but more often through the restless, agitated and disorientated behaviour characteristic of severe intoxication or withdrawal. (DHSS, 1976)

As has already been noted, certain psychiatric conditions can predispose people to violent outbursts. One victim of such was Peter Gray, a social worker with the deaf, who worked in Southampton prior to his untimely death on Tuesday, 4 July 1978. His body was discovered by the police in the home of a deaf man. Through an interpreter, the person subsequently pleaded not guilty to murder but guilty to manslaughter on the grounds of diminished responsibility and a Hospital Order was made under Section 60, with restriction without limit of time under Section 65 of the Mental Health Act 1959. Medical examinations by two doctors approved under Section 28 of the Act had diagnosed that, in addition to profound deafness, the client was suffering from paranoid schizophrenia.

Deafness and violence

Deafness is a comprehensive diagnostic term which covers many aspects of clinical conditions, and the psychological consequences vary accordingly. One of the problems of those who suffer from early profound deafness is difficulty in the acquisition of language. This, in turn, results in poor oral communication skills so that many such handicapped persons compensate by becoming expert in manual methods of communication such as finger spelling. The effects of poor language sophistication on personality development are discussed in a paper by Dr John Denmark (1972) in which he refers to personality development depending upon

> . . . genetic and environmental factors, but so heavily do the latter weigh
> against normal development in the case of the deaf child that personality
> problems are not uncommon. Many deaf school leavers present with
> problems of behaviour and adjustment. They invariably have poor
> language and poor communication skills; they are immature, egocentric
> and lacking in foresight; they are prone to impulsive and sometimes
> aggressive behaviour. To these personalities, Basilier, a Norwegian
> psychiatrist, has given the term 'Surdophrenia' or 'Deaf mind'.

The high incidence of aggressive behaviour in the history of deaf people is worth further consideration because it does seem that social workers with the deaf may be particularly vulnerable. We were given a very vivid account of a 13 year old deaf child who, because of various difficulties in his home, had to be brought into the care of his local authority. He was a young man who was physically well built, but lacking oral communication skills. Ordinary communication methods failed to get the boy out of the house where he was living and, even though the social worker appears to have been very patient and understanding, the sudden attack with a knife was unexpected and, fortunately, overcome without severe physical trauma. The result could easily have been different.

Deaf people who also suffer from dysphasia (an impediment in speaking due to impairment of cerebral function in the central nervous system) are likely to experience frustration which, in turn, may produce anger and aggression. The person's perception of the situation as well as his personality will help to decide whether violence is then precipitated or avoided.

A lack of verbal skills is an important factor in situations where there is a risk of violence. Most people will be able to discuss a difficulty, perhaps aggressively, but where there are poor verbal skills this might increase the tendency to resolve a problem by physical means. It seems likely that many potentially violent people in fact want help and have the capacity to be taught to respond to their emotions by talking rather than acting on them. With deaf people this may only be possible through sign language. Altschuler (1962) noted a predominance of disturbed behaviour in the deaf and, in a later study Denmark (1966) obtained similar findings which he considered as 'probably the result of the emotional and social immaturity of the deaf combined with their inability to "act out" verbally . . . the inability in the deaf to express dissatisfaction or anger in the normal way, or quickly enough, by emotionally toned verbalization, often leads to the physical display of such feelings'. Similar findings were documented in a later study by Denmark and Eldridge (1969).

Paranoia as a symptom in some patients suffering from deafness may be more common than the limited documented evidence might suggest.

In a survey carried out by Bute in 1979 in Bristol, there were some examples of deaf clients being suspicious and occasionally violent to each other. It has to be remembered that violence is not a frequent happening. Some local authorities have made careful provision for the needs of deaf people and, although there is no supporting scientific evidence, it seems likely that good social work support as well as sensitively planned and operated residential and day care facilities help to lessen the frustrations and practical problems associated with deafness.

When violence is threatened

Occasionally verbal threats of violence are accompanied by the production of a weapon. In cases of unpremeditated violence this is likely to be something lying on a desk or table such as scissors or a jam jar; such weapons are capable of inflicting serious injuries by someone intent on doing harm. It is essential to take threats of violence very seriously and defuse the situation whilst ensuring that precautions are taken to thwart an attack. The intentions of the violent person will be even more clear if and when a concealed weapon is suddenly produced. Whilst there is an undoubted need to remain calm and not panic, the production of a weapon must always be taken seriously. People respond differently to such situations and it is therefore difficult to be precise about the way in which to respond to emergencies of this nature, but in Chapter 5 we shall attempt to answer the question of what to do if violence occurs.

It is sometimes difficult for people to grasp fully the

significance of what is happening to them when confronted by aggressive behaviour which verges on violence. In most of us there is a reactive denial mechanism of 'It's not going to happen to me!' or 'I must be dreaming! Sit tight and I shall wake up from the nightmare in five minutes!' Even though they may sometimes seem trivial, all clear threats of violence should be taken seriously. Sometimes, this will be the only outward sign that a person is potentially violent. Staff members should not overreact to the extent that an inappropriate response inadvertently precipitates a violent reaction, but it is equally important that early warning signals are quickly identified and met with an appropriate response.

Potential causes

Whilst it is necessary to try to anticipate violence, care should be taken to avoid labelling a person to the extent that he or she has to live up to those expectations. For many staff this is a dilemma. On the one hand history is the best predictor, on the other there is the danger of it becoming a self-fulfilling prophecy.

> . . . it does seem that boys who have been violent before are expected by staff to be violent again, and so frequently are. Almost half the boys concerned in violent incidents in one of the schools we studied had been previously involved more than once, suggesting that expectations can render conflict more likely and more fierce. Unfortunately, it is not possible to trace the parallel violent histories of adults in the schools, although there is considerable evidence that certain staff are more likely to be involved in violent acts than others. (Millham *et al.*, 1978, p. 62)

These comments of Millham, Bullock and Hosie are worthy of note because of the influence of 'labelling' and also because of the point they make about staff involvement. If this is the case, then there are implications for staff recruitment and selection procedures, and we shall be giving further consideration to this in the next chapter.

Unexpected violence

Not all violence is pre-meditated and, in some instances, it is impossible to recognise potential violence or anticipate it. Dr Frank Wells (1983) a general practitioner, illustrates this point from personal experience.

Hamlet Jones was an odd chap; he had first registered with me more than 18 months earlier, and his notes and the treatment with which he arrived confirmed a diagnosis of schizophrenia. He had attended the surgery on each of the following four days after his registration – on all of them just to make sure I was still there. Thereafter he had behaved in a mildly irrational but docile manner, frequently attending the surgery with trivial complaints. He came six times in each of the next two months, twice the following month, and then once a month for nearly a year, presumably because he was satisfied with himself. When he came again he told me that he had moved to Felixstowe, over 12 miles away, so I had to advise him to change doctors. He was very agitated and depressed at the time, however, and this advice made him worse. So I kept him on the list for a while, and with the help of the social workers, support from me, and the appropriate drug treatment he succeeded in getting back to work. That was in July and until November he stayed in the same job – quite an achievement for him.

The next time he appeared in the surgery was to tell me how upset he was that the council would not let him stay with his mother in Felixstowe; this was probably a cock-and-bull story, but we next read in the local paper that Hamlet had recently assaulted two Social Security officers, so I was alerted to his history of aggression. Hamlet, however had never been physically aggressive to me or anyone else at the health centre, and his appearance that morning was nothing surprising. Hamlet had arrived while I was out visiting, but although appointments were full he knew he could wait and be fitted in. My partners left him to me because I knew him.

Four patients with appointments came first, and one of my partners had a chat with me in between two of them before he went out on his visits. I knew, however, that he was dealing with some papers in his consulting room before he set off. In came Hamlet, bright as a button, but calm and relaxed – or so I believed, 'Have a seat,' seemed a reasonable greeting to give him, but what followed was totally unreasonable.

I do not actually remember what happened next, but apparently Hamlet crashed my head against the top of my own desk, stunning me momentarily, and breaking my glasses. My partner, separated by two closed doors and two examination rooms, happened to come out of his room to set off on his visits, heard the kerfuffle, and came into my room. I was protecting myself from a further head-battering by disappearing under the desk – or I may have fallen there, because I still do not remember any of the episode. Hamlet decided to destroy my watch and my coat while he was about it, my partner somehow alerted the receptionists, and police and ambulance men arrived without delay. Meanwhile, however, Hamlet made off.

This is an unusual case but is by no means the only recorded one of its kind. A similarly vivid example is provided by probation officer Arthur Caiger, who lost his sight following an assault by a man whose identity is still not known.

On Friday 1st December 1978, about 20 past 9 the 'phone rang and one of my daughters answered it. The person asked for me, so I went to the 'phone and said 'Hello', and there was no answer. About 20 minutes later the doorbell rang and, when it was answered by my daughter, there stood on the doorstep a young man with a crash helmet and motor cycling gear. He asked for me and I sent a message downstairs to ask him to come in; (it was a very cold winter in 1978) my daughter came upstairs again and said 'No he hasn't got time for that', so I came downstairs and I found a man standing in the hall; with his left hand he raised the visor of his crash helmet and, with his right hand he threw some hydrochloric acid into my face. I was immediately blinded of course and my daughter ran out. I'm not quite sure what she thought she could do, but she saw him running up the road to meet another chap at the top who was clearly the instigator of the event. Of course, had I recognised the man, that would have meant his courting disaster. The chap who threw the acid was not one of my clients but one of the men coming out of prison told me that someone had been paid to do it. There is still no clear reason why it should have happened. I had been at Richmond for 18 years and then I was sent to the Crown Court at Kingston where I did not have a caseload; there have never been any arrests for the assault and the reason for it has never been made clear. The assumption is that I had put in a report on someone who had had to be sent down, but it could have been all sorts of things. The motive was never substantiated.

Given hindsight, I could not have done anything differently. I have been a probation officer for 20 years. Clearly not everyone liked me and there were a few who were capable of assaulting me in that way and there were one or two who I thought disliked me sufficiently to want to harm me. There had been a previous occasion . . . in May 1975 a paraffin soaked rag was pressed through the letter box and set fire to, and exactly one month later the same thing happened again.

The common elements in the two accounts centre on the fact that violence was not anticipated and, thus could not be prevented.

It is impossible to know everything about the people who arrive at offices, attend day centres, or live in residential establishments and sometimes it is very difficult to recognise potential violence. In a London bail hostel, for instance, adult males over 17 years of age are received from the courts as an alternative to a remand in custody. The Warden, Dennis Powell, is a senior Probation Officer and has talked about problems of violence in this type of residence, where staff appear to be very much at risk because of the absence of residents' previous case histories (Powell, 1983).

Behaviour and mood changes

There will be instances when the medical or social history is known and indicates a low tolerance of frustration and a problem of violent behaviour. For example, one would expect Hamlet Jones' current GP to take a slightly different approach now that there is the benefit of previous history and case record. Note must always be taken of early warning signs and symptoms of potential violence, and it is important to examine these against the background of previous knowledge of the person's medical history as well as social behaviour. Residential and day care staff who spend long periods of time with people should develop an ability to interpret the significance of particular behavioural and mood changes. This is especially true in establishments for the mentally handicapped and mentally ill. The onset of catatonic features such as posturing and mutism might be warning signs of violence in someone suffering from schizophrenia. Staff working in old people's homes will be familiar with the occasional aggressive if not violent outburst from a resident. This is more likely to happen at night when unfamiliar surroundings, darkness and a degree of dementia occasionally appear to combine to produce bizarre symptoms of confusion, paranoia and aggression.

In such circumstances, failure to observe and listen to the

resident can aggravate the problem. One such occasion arose in a residential establishment for the elderly when a newly admitted man was being attended to by two female members of staff. He did not understand and certainly did not appreciate their attempts to be friendly and welcoming; indeed, he appeared to resent them and his attutude changed from marked hostility to aggressive language until he was on the verge of becoming violent. In due course, the resident was approached by a junior male member of staff who quietly asked what the matter was. 'I need the loo . . .' was the immediate reply of a man who had, seemingly, been too embarrassed to enquire of his earlier attendants.

We are unable to confirm or deny that violent acts in our society are increasing, but we are aware of considerable concern being expressed by various professional agencies during the past few years. Police and Health Authorities, as well as Probation, Education and Social Services Departments have a need to recognise potential violence so as to intervene at the earliest possible stage.

Millham, Bullock and Hosie have also concluded that offences sometimes seem to cluster at particular times, depending upon such things as changes in the leading group. Because there were so few serious incidents in their study, it was not possible to identify the existence of cycles but there might be a few agencies where violence is sufficient of a problem that charting events could be worthwhile and potentially significant (Millham *et al.*, 1978, p. 61).

Conclusions

Recognising potential violence is sometimes possible, especially in establishments that are geared to identifying and diagnosing medical conditions like those we have referred to in this chapter. There is a need to observe, listen and record as well as to take serious account of the threat of violence whenever it is made. We should always anticipate but, at the same time, avoid labelling people in such a way that violence becomes a self-fulfilling prophecy. Sometimes it will be impossible to anticipate, because the violent act is not always premeditated and does not always have an obvious cause; at all times, the major endeavour should be to stop relationships deteriorating. Occasionally, we can anticipate violence arising in certain situations, especially where deprivation of liberty is a predominant factor. In Chapter 6 we shall consider how to minimise the damage if violence should occur, but first we must look at prevention.

Points for practice

- Factors associated with violence include isolation, stress and violent experiences in a person's own childhood. Contributory factors include the disinhibiting effects of alcohol and certain drugs.
- Situations associated with violence include the taking of children into care under Place of Safety orders, formal hospital admissions under the Mental Health Act, and to a lesser extent the taking of elderly people into care under the National Assistance Act. These are all situations involving the deprivation of liberty.
- Some psychotic states are associated with violence.
- Deafness and its attendant frustrations may be associated with violence.
- All threats of violence should be taken seriously.
- Production of a weapon should always be taken seriously.
- A person's medical or social history may indicate a low tolerance of frustration and a potential for violence.
- Managers and staff should discuss and decide on appropriate action in situations where potential violence is identified. In such situations, it may be prudent to annotate case records.
- Staff should develop the ability to interpret behaviour and mood changes.
- It is important to observe, listen and record; but 'labelling' should be avoided.

4

Preventing Violence

Although problems exist in any attempt to predict dangerousness (see for example Floud and Young, 1983), efforts must be made to plan to reduce or prevent violence. There is need for careful consideration of techniques and methods used in all work centres. Managers will need to give special attention to the calibre of staff appointed to key positions, as well as to their training needs. It does seem to us that as other professions have experienced violence in the past, social work agencies should be taking note of advice given to staff in hospitals. In particular, nursing and medical staff in this country as well as overseas have made the major contribution to the limited amount of available literature.

Identifying the circumstances in which violence might occur and the characteristics of people who are likely to be aggressive should make it possible to reduce the number of violent incidents. Violence must always be dealt with in a competent manner, using skills which should be discussed and developed in training programmes which are geared to need.

Interviewing and reception arrangements

Sometimes, very simple straightforward precautions can be taken in order to avoid violence. Problems of communication between staff must be overcome in order to provide good information which will assist all who take part in planning procedures and methods of working.

There are also points to be kept in mind which are practical and should not be spurned because of their apparent simplicity. For example, the importance of *feeling* physically safe in one's role should not be underestimated. If staff feel secure with potentially violent people, they are more likely to handle difficult interviews appropriately and without mishap. A sense of security might be provided, for example, by arranging for someone to 'stand-by' and listen in to the conversation outside the interviewing room door, so that help can be immediately available in the event of an emergency. The tone of a conversation can be noted quite easily, especially if and when voices are raised in anger and with threats. Some agencies find it helpful to make discreet, and sometimes 'coded', arrangements so that the receptionist, or another member of staff, interrupts or investigates an interview if it is felt that things are getting out of hand. The interruption might extract the interviewer from a tight situation, or it may provide an opportunity for reassurance that all is well. For example, an interview may be interrupted intentionally by a colleague who apologises and then asks the interviewer if a moment can be spared for conversation outside the room. Once outside, assistance can be arranged if it is needed.

Some agencies have verbal 'codes' which are used in telephoning for help without alarming or alerting a potentially violent person. For instance, staff in a London probation office have predetermined that if the switchboard gets a request from a probation officer to check whether he has inadvertently left his car lights switched on, this is in fact an indication that he needs help.

It is to be hoped that departments will be able to avoid the arrangements that many Supplementary Benefit offices have had to make, with chairs and tables secured to the floor and elaborate screens. Nevertheless, it makes sense if potential weapons such as heavy ash-trays are discreetly hidden or, alternatively, designed in such a way as to make them less dangerous. Similarly, it is likely to be helpful if seating can be arranged so that the interviewer is positioned near to the door or one of the two alarm buttons which should be located on opposite sides of the interviewing room. (These same buttons should be of the type that only cancel from a point outside the interviewing room.)

It is often at this simple level that things go wrong and violence occurs. For example, in one particular office, well known to us, where staff pride themselves in having thought through many of these issues, a social worker was left to interview a visitor to the area office at the end of a working day. Soon afterwards, everyone left the office without checking that the social worker was all right. As it happened, all was well, but a check made by those leaving the building at five p.m. should be as automatic as ensuring that all windows and doors are closed. Receptionist staff should alert the line manager to the fact that staff are still interviewing.

By definition, many of the people who come to social services and probation departments have personal problems which are causing them anxiety and distress. This in turn may lead them to behave irrationally and could, on occasion, help to precipitate violent reactions. It is, therefore, incumbent upon agencies to ensure that all visitors are received courteously and compassionately by staff who are sensitive and understanding. Many departments take care to appoint excellent receptionists and telephonists, and professional training is then sometimes provided for the important role they are to undertake. Regrettably, salaries paid to these staff are not always commensurate with the vital duties they undertake.

Hall found in his research that some receptionists and the conditions under which reception interviews were conducted were far from ideal;

> Clients were expected to explain their request to the receptionist on duty in a room which was often crowded with other waiting clients. The opportunities for privacy in such a situation were necessarily limited, especially when the staff failed to see this as a problem. In one instance of many which could be quoted, a receptionist called across a crowded room to a client, 'When did your wife leave you, Mr-?' This lack of confidentiality could be seen to produce anxiety and distress for a sizeable proportion of the clients interviewed. (Hall. 1974, p. 62)

Physiological factors

In addition to the circumstances in which people are received and interviewed, there may be physiological explanations for their aggressive behaviour. From time to time biochemical research has indicated a relationship between certain foods, the body's physiological processes and particular medical conditions. David Woodman has claimed that true psychopaths act the way they do because of an imbalance in the adrenal glands. In a paper given at the 22nd Annual Conference of the Society of Psychosomatic Research in London in 1978, Woodman is reported as saying:

> There would appear to be a group of subjects who are identifiable as being biochemically abnormal in their adrenal response to anticipatory stress, lacking in physiological responsivity to stressful stimuli and having a history of convictions for serious aggressive behaviour . . . these, I would contend, are the true psychopaths and this has important implications, if true, for diagnosis and treatment. (Woodman, 1979)

We are not competent to comment on these claims or Woodman's opinion, but at the most simple psychological and physiological levels, it might well be helpful to provide a cup of tea at a time when things seem to be getting out of control. This can sometimes create a very practical opportunity for staff to demonstrate goodwill and a desire to help. Very occasionally there may be practical reasons which cause a person to be violent, such as lack of food as well as money. A cup of tea with sugar will sometimes help to prevent confrontation, although some discernment will be necessary to ensure that the hot drink is not itself used as a weapon.

Sylvia Woolfe has worked in the field of health care for many years. As group principal social worker at University Hospital, Nottingham, she emphasises the need to be aware of how a person's physical functioning can affect their behaviour and attitude:

> I can remember, a long time ago, when I first started my social work career as a marriage guidance counsellor, interviewing a client one evening about his complex marital problems. For about an hour the discussion had been rational and reasonably objective, when suddenly, and for no apparent reason my client became very excited and aggressive, raised his voice, paced the room, and in short exhibited such irrational and, to me, inexplicable behaviour, that my only concern was to bring the interview to a close as speedily as possible.

Recounting this later to a colleague, better informed than I about medical matters, he immediately enquired, 'Did he happen to be diabetic?' I looked at him as though he were clairvoyant; in fact, the client had told me early on in our conversation that he was indeed diabetic, but I had not made the connection between that and his sudden and violent outburst. Presumably the stress of the situation, coupled with the fact that he had not eaten for some time, had affected his metabolism – the offer of a biscuit might have been more helpful than my soothing word! (Woolfe, 1984)

Identifying potential triggers

Basing his comments on work with mentally handicapped people in hospital, Hope (1973) refers to the need for staff to build relationships and to study behaviour patterns. With this knowledge, outbursts and emotional upsets can be prevented by the recognition of 'trigger factors', so called because they are responsible for triggering emotional explosions, including violent episodes (see Chapter 2). They take many forms and might include: 'excess noise such as other patients screaming, or loud radio music, it may well be the way that another person is looking at the patient; he may have cornflakes instead of porridge for breakfast . . .'.

Sometimes, says Hope, the trigger response is obscure and detailed research into the patient's daily life is needed to find the reason. This point is illustrated with an account of a 57 year old male patient with a mental age of 2½ years, 4ft 10 ins in height and of slight build. His speech was very limited and he had paralysis of the left arm and left leg. Despite this physical handicap he was quite mobile;

He has developed no close friendships but displays an affection towards most of the female staff and identifies them with his mother. He also sublimates affections through the medium of an old rag doll or teddy bear . . . Recently took an intense dislike to one of the newly qualified SENs. He was verbally rude to her and attempted to strike her on several occasions. On one such occasion the Charge Nurse intervened and, in spite of his physical handicap, Ginger displayed great violence. At the time of the assault, he was in bed and the Charge Nurse leaned over to talk to him about his dislike of the female nurse. Ginger then suddenly grabbed the Charge Nurse by the hair and hit him several times in the face with sufficient force to break the Charge Nurse's glasses, knock his dentures out of alignment, and cause cuts and bruises about his face . . .

An on-the-spot ward meeting was held . . . [and] Ginger's recent behaviour pattern was discussed in detail and no reason for his dislike of the young SEN could be found . . . The meeting was on the verge of breaking up when the Nursing Officer said she had not seen the dirty old rag doll lately and wondered what had happened to it. Most of the nurses did not know but the young SEN in question said that because the doll was dirty and unhygienic she had taken it away from him . . . q.e.d.

A thorough knowledge of potential trigger factors can best be obtained in work places where there are opportunities for staff discussion and where there are good channels of communication between staff members. Systematic recording of significant incidents is particularly important where a system of different shifts is used to cover 24 hour periods. In day centres where staff sometimes work in different workshops, and in residential centres, it can be difficult to maintain good relationships and clear communication, but it is essential that staff teams work together to achieve this objective. Sometimes, in discussion with the line manager, it will be possible for staff to admit to being afraid; admission of fear can be very useful and should never be seen as failure.

Planning ahead

It will also be necessary for staff to spend time with the line manager in discussing methods to be used in approaching potentially violent situations. On occasion, for example, it will be necessary to decide whether to visit on a domiciliary basis in pairs rather than individually. It might be more prudent to ask the person to make an appointment for an interview at the area office. If things are likely to be particularly difficult, such as is sometimes the case with formal admissions under the Mental Health Act or removing a child under the provisions of a Place of Safety Order, it will be necessary to ask for police assistance. This might be in token form – one officer waiting outside in case help is required – or with sufficient numbers to provide adequate and effective protection. Professional judgement will determine the optimum police presence, but the escalating effects of a large number of police personnel together should be kept in mind.

In order to obtain appropriate urgent assistance it is necessary to have a clear understanding of the role of the police as well as the local interpretation of standing orders. Good relationships will aid communication and help the police to respond appropriately when called upon to intervene urgently.

When escorting in cars, it will sometimes be necessary to make use of child-proof door locks in order to avoid the risk of anyone attempting to get out of a moving vehicle. It is best to ensure that, whenever possible, the person being conveyed is sitting in the rear seat. The accompanying escort should sit immediately behind the driver, and will then be well placed to protect him in the event of a disturbance. If there is any doubt about a passenger's predictability, a second escort should be present or, better still, arrangements should be made for transport by ambulance.

Staff characteristics

In the context of violence prevention, it is essential that managers give careful consideration to the qualities needed by the person they are looking for at the time of staff recruitment. It is often in this area of responsibility that the seeds of difficulty are first sown. We have already noted that Millham *et al.* refer to considerable evidence that certain staff are more likely to be involved in violent acts than others (1978, p. 68). Staff members were responsible for provoking violence in two-thirds of examined incidents in their research project, and were the ones who hit first. The authors go on to say that: 'Those whose task it is to establish the exact dynamics of violent incidents such as lawyers or administrators in the Criminal Injuries Compensation Board, comment that it is often difficult to decide who is the assailant and who is the victim when all the circumstances are reviewed.'

There is a need for all staff members to be selected carefully, but more especially when they are likely to be in contact with people from outside the agency. Sometimes this will be face to face contact such as exists between fieldworker and client or receptionist and visitor, but administrative staff who have telephone conversations with enquirers are also key personnel in that they represent the initial point of contact with a department, and it is often at this time that attitudes and future relationships are determined.

Good interviewing techniques usually ensure the appointment of staff whose approach and personalities help to prevent violence rather than cause it. It might occasionally be necessary to acknowledge an inappropriate appointment, or that the person appointed lacks certain attributes or expertise which, at the time of interview, were not noticeably absent. Attention should be given to in-service training programmes which will help to overcome identified needs. Appropriate programmes will be part of the syllabus of all progressive departments and may well include the sort of video training materials currently being marketed. Line managers who are responsible for identifying training needs will also want to consider the advisability of transferring staff whose presentation and general demeanour is going to continue to cause relationship problems despite intensive training. Hopefully, this will seldom be necessary.

Regimes

During the past few years there has been a move away from an authoritarian approach in residential and day care sectors. This has been especially evident in local authority establishments, as well as in some centres for penal reform. Whatmore, for example, tells of a special unit for ten prisoners that was set up in Scotland in 1973 (Whatmore, 1983). The traditional paternalistic officer–inmate relationship was dispensed with in favour of a therapist–patient approach. This entailed a breakdown of established attitudes among staff who had been previously trained on the principle that officers do not talk to inmates. It was expected that difficult situations would arise, not least because of the history of violent offences for which the inmates had been convicted. In order to defuse potentially difficult situations, it was decided, from the start, that anyone (inmate or officer) could convene a 'community meeting' in order to talk about problems. Everyone was encouraged to express their own opinion and, after an initial hesitancy, the meetings gradually became more constructive. A person was elected to chair each meeting: minutes were kept and decisions were made democratically, except for proposals that would influence the security of the unit.

At the start there was an 'us:them' barrier, but the two groups gradually began to work towards goals which were mutually acceptable. There was increasing freedom to criticise peers on both sides. In addition to regular weekly meetings of this nature, emergency meetings could be convened and these were invaluable in coping with phantasies and misunderstandings. Both groups became increasingly able to talk about their phantasies and create a corporate sense of identity and responsibility. It was not a psychotherapeutic group; neither was the communication in any way psychodynamic; in fact, at times, the language used was very basic!

Antisocial behaviour was brought to the notice of the group; facts were established and action was then decided. Unacceptable behaviour by staff and/or inmates was dealt with and there was usually a sense of fairness. Barriers between staff and inmates became less evident, whilst opinions were openly expressed, ventilating hostility and aggression. Whilst the overall effect was of a positive nature, it should also be noted that some staff members and inmates experienced difficulty in coming to terms with criticism. Some felt very threatened and feared their own hostility and aggression; several in the group became aware of its destructive power against individuals. On the whole, however, this appears to have been a very positive contribution to the prevention of violence in one specialised agency, and has many similarities to the regime that has been successfully developed at Grendon Psychiatric Prison in Buckinghamshire.

In a completely different situation Ronald Wiener, a Psychiatric day centre manager for Leeds City Council, stresses the need to make members feel it is their centre;

> Two things follow from this, members will help to make sure the centre is a pleasant place to be, and if they determine the way the centre is run then whatever rules that there are will have been agreed by everyone rather than imposed arbitrarily by the staff.

Rule breaking then becomes a matter of concern to everyone rather than a struggle for power between staff and members. In practice it means that most centre members will help to defuse situations and support each other in ensuring rules are enforced. (Wiener, 1983)

The matter of relationships is obviously of importance. Inexperienced and unqualified staff may inadvertently exacerbate problems. Sometimes a staff member will be incompatible with someone and there may well be a need for the manager to assess the situation carefully and determine whether changes can be made in order to ease the difficulty. This can be seen as 'failure' and staff members are likely to need support in coming to terms with adjustments of this nature. In a day centre, this might mean moving the instructor to a different work group; in an area office it might mean transferring a particular case to a different worker. In large residential establishments it will sometimes be necessary to arrange shifts and work schedules so that certain staff have little or no contact with particular residents. Clearly, the smaller the home the more difficult the solution; the only possibility might be to remove either the offender or the offended to a different residential establishment. Although this is likely to happen only in extreme cases, it should certainly be kept in mind as an available option.

Training

A considerable number of health authorities, social services departments and social work training establishments are now giving increasing thought to the inclusion of training material which suitably reflects the need to help people cope with a problem which has been largely neglected or ignored in the past. From the Bristol survey (Bute, 1979a) as well as the Wessex study it was evident that, in 1979–80 there was very little guidance on violence available for staff in vocational training in its widest sense, including professional training courses and 'in service' programmes. Of the 338 respondents in Wessex, 57 (17 per cent) replied in the affirmative to the question 'In your vocational training (in its widest sense including "in service" and "on the job" training), were you given any guidance in the practical management of violence?'

276 (82 per cent) replied negatively and 5 did not know. Training is so crucial to the successful prevention of violence that we shall comprehensively examine the issues in Chapter 8.

Employers' expectations and responsibilities

Most of the social workers interviewed in the Bristol survey agreed with the hypothesis that training courses expect social workers to 'casework' aggression rather than retreat from it. We also suspect this to be true of social services departments where, in the past, little or no consideration appears to have been given to the question of what to do if cornered in a room by an aggressive person brandishing a knife. Whilst this is not a frequent occurrence, for a few it could literally be their first and last encounter. Given the evidence of actual injuries during the past few years this is by no means alarmist. Peter Gray died whilst providing community care for a paranoid deaf and dumb client; in November 1974 Murray Bruggen, later chairman of the National Association of Probation Officers, received brain damage following an assault which took place in his own office, the aggressor was an alcoholic; in 1978 a female probation officer, Pat Watling, was stabbed by a drug-abusing client during a home visit; in 1978 a male probation officer, Arthur Caiger, lost his sight after an acid attack at his home. In 1984 a hospital social worker, Isobel Schwarz, was stabbed to death in her office. In 1985, Peter Durrant was severely injured in a road accident whilst trying to escort a patient to psychiatric hospital.

From an in-service training point of view, an employer's general duty under the 1974 Health and Safety at Work Act is to provide a safe system of work. The Act also places a duty on the employer to provide 'such information, instruction, training and supervision as is necessary to ensure, so far as is reasonably practicable, the safety at work of his employees' (Section 2(2) (C)).

Millham *et al.* are of the opinion that, at least in the residential establishments where their research took place, almost all staff – boy conflicts were entirely avoidable;

Unfortunately, it seems that few staff have had even the simplest instructions on how to take preventive action. Frequently they hasten into confrontations in which neither staff nor boy feels he can back down without significant loss of face. Such confrontation often takes place in group situations where the esteem of others will be lost by backing down and, inevitably, the chances of an aggressive response are heightened . . . Yet, people can be trained to avoid violence, either by side-stepping the confrontation or by meeting it in much the same way as violent patients are contained in mental hospitals. It is unfortunate that few of these strategies ever form part of the courses offered to students destined for posts in schools or residential homes (1978, p. 64).

Health Service experiences

For those of us directly or indirectly involved in work with the personal social services, the problem of how best to prevent violence is not a new one; neither is it an issue that has become easier nor more difficult to deal with. It is worth noting, however, that related agencies have experienced similar problems and there is much to be gained from a brief examination of some of their difficulties as well as the attempts which have been made to overcome them.

Health agencies in general, and psychiatric hospitals in particular, have had to give very serious thought to the prevention of violence during the past few years. In 1974, State Enrolled Nurse Daniel Carey was stabbed to death by a schizophrenic patient at Tooting Bec Hospital, London; in the same year a nurse from Coventry Hospital was beaten up by a patient and had to take three weeks off work. In May 1978, again at Tooting Bec Hospital, Ward Sister Elisabeth Carson was killed by a 22 year old male patient. In June 1978, a nurse was awarded £20 000 by the Criminal Injuries Compensation Board; she had been attacked by a drunken man in June 1969. Medicine is also a high risk profession; during the two year period from May 1976 to 1978, in Great Britain, a general practitioner was killed and two consultants, one a psychiatrist and the other a general physician, were gravely injured by mentally disturbed patients.

These are, of course, some of the extreme cases that come to the notice of the media. One suspects that there are many more which, for various reasons, remain unpublicised and therefore unrecorded. Currently, a Health Services Advisory Committee working party on violence against National Health Service staff has been set up and, in due course, it hopes to send a list of recommendations to central government and, if necessary, to issue guidelines on how best to manage and prevent violence.

Dr John Wall of the Medical Defence Union says he hears from GPs suffering the effects of an assault about once a week and in his career he has dealt with three cases where doctors have been killed by their patients.

A vivid example is provided by Dr Alan Manch, a single-handed GP who works in a particularly rundown part of south London.

He is proud of the fact that he will treat anybody, and says that several of his patients are drug addicts, winos and tramps.

He worked without a receptionist until a man pulled out a knife demanding drugs. This incident prompted him not only to employ a receptionist, but to have an alarm system rigged from the surgery to the reception area.

'I have been threatened repeatedly but this made me really frightened. I now have a receptionist for protection. She has a lock on her door and can call the flying squad immediately I sound the alarm,' he says.

The problem is not confined to Britain. Articles in the nursing press from other countries provide interesting perspectives from different angles; Lillian Stegne, writing in 'Canadian Nurse' (1978) has detailed the results of a programme at a psychiatric hospital where, after implementation of the programme, it was claimed that incidents of disturbed behaviour decreased significantly and patient injuries as well as patient-related staff injuries also decreased. This latter article is well illustrated with pictures detailing methods of release from various physical attacks, as well as techniques for physical restraint.

Philip Penningroth (1975) and Anne Marie De Felippo (1976), both from the USA, have provided helpful contributions. Penningroth, whilst accepting the need for physical restraint in certain instances, calls for a well organised and co-ordinated policy on the control of violence. He argues that physical force should not be used to control violence, except as a last resort, and then only if the patient is actually violent. Most people would agree with that, as well as two later suggestions of techniques of control;

> Interacting with the patient [which] involves the abilities to be warm and empathetic, to communicate clearly to help the patient distinguish reality and come to some understanding of his own behaviour, and to be kind but firm in setting limits.
>
> Talking is the single most effective way to help a patient gain self-control and should be used increasingly in violent situations. When interacting, it is important to be aware of body posture and position and to try to stand or sit in a way that will be least threatening to the patient.

After giving an illustration of an assault by a 23 year old psychotic male patient on a female nurse, De Felippo explores the background to the incident and forcibly argues that it could have been prevented by observing basic ground rules:

1. The need to maintain a degree of physical distance.
2. Importance of alarm buttons especially in seclusion rooms.
3. The need to note important behavioural clues given by the patient.
4. Importance of a knowledge of a patient's previous history, especially cases in which violent episodes can be identified.
5. The need to make it clear to the patient that control will be maintained by the staff and that certain sanctions will be applied in the event of destructive behaviour.
6. Importance of physical activity as a channel for directing aggression.
7. Staff are valued for the sense of humour they are able to provide when tension begins to mount on the unit.
8. In-service training programmes.
9. The need for staff to feel comfortable in caring for patients whose impulse control is poor.

In the UK, the 'Nursing Times' (17 November 1977, pp. 1982–3) published a news feature of a film and booklet produced in conjunction with the South East Thames Regional Health Authority on the Nursing management of violence and violent patients. The article, like Stegne's, is well illustrated with photographs showing how to deal with personal attacks. Mostly, however, the nursing press in this country has published articles of a more general nature on the subject. Harrington (1972), a psychiatrist, wrote that 'more often than not violence in hospitals is a symptom of a disturbance in the hospital itself rather than a symptom of a patient's particular mental state' whilst Coffey (1976), following the enquiries into the Ely, Farleigh and South Ockendon Hospitals, stated that 'no-one now questions the fact that overcrowding, under-staffing, poor leadership and weak management all predispose to conditions which impose additional strains on the for-bearance of staff and patients alike'. Coffey's article is important, not least because it provides a very balanced survey of the nursing literature available on the subject at the time of writing. Although we have progressed since that time, many of the problems remain unresolved and departmental managers might do well to examine some of the findings of earlier researchers. Brailsford and Stevenson, for example (1973), conducted an enquiry at Mapperley and St Ann's Hospitals into the kind of disturbed situation that might be precipitated by hospital environment or the inter-relationship between staff, and between staff and patients. As charge nurses in the psychiatric hospital, they found that conditions contributed to a high level of stress and anxiety among the nursing staff which, in turn, led to their adopting the kind of inflexible behaviour which characterises authoritarian relationships.

Conclusions

In this chapter, we have sought to outline ways in which much violence can be prevented. We have tried to be practical and several of the simple precautions which have been set out in the first part of the chapter will already be second nature to many staff, whether practitioners or managers. They are included because it is sometimes helpful to remind ourselves what precautions need to be taken. Other aspects are partly philosophical and we have attempted to show by illustration that a move away from an authoritarian approach is likely to produce a climate in which the seeds of violence fail to germinate. Other agencies, (mainly health authorities) and other countries (nurses from the USA and Canada) have provided examples of ways in which we might develop our thinking and approach to the problem in the UK. We have much to learn from these sources; it is, unfortunately, a fact of life that violence will still occur even when all the lessons have been learnt.

Points for practice

- Planning for the reduction of violence is a task for managers to undertake with their staff.
- Staff should feel secure in their work. This might be made possible, for example, by the proximity of a 'stand-by' person, by pre-arranged interruptions, or by the use of verbal telephone 'codes' requesting assistance, as well as by conventional alarm systems.
- Objects with potential as weapons should not be left lying around.
- Interviewers should be within reach of alarm systems.
- Staff should not be left alone in a building.
- Callers should always be received courteously.
- All staff, including receptionists and telephonists, should receive in-service training in the management of potential violence.
- Reception arrangements should afford privacy to callers.
- An offer of a warm drink may be useful in some situations.
- Staff should be sensitive to 'trigger factors'.
- In residential and day centres, significant events should be recorded.
- Staff should feel able to admit to being afraid at times.
- The kind of decisions made by managers and staff might include, for example, paired home visits, supervised office interviews, and the obtaining of discreet police assistance in appropriate cases.
- Agencies should develop good relationships with the police.
- When recruiting staff, care should be taken to avoid the appointment of people who may precipitate or provoke violence.
- In residential and day centres, paternalistic and authoritarian regimes should be reconsidered.

- Incompatibilities between individual staff and residents should be reviewed with care.
- Heightened confrontations should be sidestepped or otherwise avoided.
- Talking with potentially violent people is important.
- Adopting a non-threatening posture is important.
- Maintaining a physical distance is important.
- Physical activity may provide a useful channel for redirecting aggression.
- Humour can usefully defuse tension.

5

If Violence Occurs...

The time will come, especially in settings where there are potentially violent people, when violence occurs even though appropriate staff responses have been made and all possible action taken to prevent such occurrences. Some people live with such a short tolerance fuse that it is impossible to avoid the occasional explosion. It also needs to be acknowledged that we all make mistakes. There will be times when something inappropriate is said or done which is sufficient to trigger a violent response. In the context of violence towards staff in Probation and Social Services, it is necessary to remember that violence is not a day to day experience. It does happen, however, and correct methods of dealing with it are, of course, extremely important. Badly handled violence will lead to people being injured emotionally as well as physically.

Immediate action

Most potentially violent situations can be defused by keeping control and observing practical guidelines. This does sometimes mean that the staff member has the dilemma of deciding which method of intervention, if any, to choose, as is well illustrated from Dennis Powell's experience:

> During the first year or so at Balham, I had no deputy and with only three staff it was not possible to cover all the hours without me doing an additional shift and working Friday night in addition to five days. On one such Friday night, I was physically attacked, the one and only time in my career, although I have, of course, been threatened many times.

We had in the Hostel at that time a vicious youth, with a history of violence and unpredictable behaviour. One of those who fall between the legal and psychiatric provisions. He had, already threatened other members of staff in ways that, with the experience I have now, would make me get rid of him at a much earlier stage in the interests of staff safety . . .

. . . this lad had threatened other members of staff but clearly I was the number one target and he waited until the Friday night when I was on duty to make his move. He came to the office around 11.30 p.m. saying he wanted to talk with me and from the beginning he adopted a hostile manner. As is my style in such situations, I remained calm, softly spoken and concealed any apprehension I was feeling. The real trouble started when I tried to bring the talk to a close, he refused to leave the office, I asked him to leave politely, then firmly, then decisively, but he would not go.

From then on I employed my whole repertoire of strategies to get him out or escape from him whilst trying to avoid increasing the violence and sustaining personal injury. I tried relaxing, sitting it out, I was, after all, on duty all night but he would then become very provocative, sweeping things off the desk, being abusive or physically menacing, grabbing me and on one occasion pulled my tie tightly round my neck. In the course of one of these scuffles I received a cut over my eye, nothing serious, probably caused by a finger nail . . . Eventually, after two or three hours, my captor seemed to tire of the game and began asking what I would do if he let me go. We bargained for a while and agreed, come the finish, to leave the office together and with the understanding that I leave the hostel. (Powell, 1983)

The importance of choosing the correct method is again well illustrated by David Pithers who, as Director of Studies in the National Children's Home, had the following experience:

With one group I arrived on the third week to find a crowd of the smaller skin-heads bullying (strange word from my respectable background but it does convey quite accurately what was happening) – one of the black lads. Because this did not appear to involve a great deal of dedication or power I intervened to stop it – and got my come-uppance. A much larger skin-head, who until then had been watching with apparent amusement, caught hold of me and dragged me out, with the assistance of some and the support of others, into the middle of the floor, where he rendered me helpless by kneeling on my shoulders and grabbing me by the throat. It is strange how a part of the mind is able to detach itself and observe what other parts are powerfully experiencing. My memory of the event is very clear, even in the tiniest details, until the point where I lost consciousness.

Subsequently I learnt that as soon as I failed to feed his violence by reacting to it he let go of me, gave me a contemptuous kick and spat at me. The consequences were both apparent when I came round. (Pithers, 1983)

These two illustrations show how difficult it is to make appropriate decisions about intervention when situations become tense and fraught. 'Should I act now or later? What if this makes him – or her – react even more aggressively?'

Physical restraint

One of the difficulties with which staff have to come to terms is the decision whether or not to use physical restraint. This is also a dilemma facing staff in special hospitals, especially following the death of Michael Martin, a patient, at Broadmoor. William Bingley, Legal Director of Mind, considers that:

The Michael Martin inquest and its aftermath has raised many issues, prominent amongst them, the use of force in special hospitals. One of the powerful aftertastes of the inquest was the impression given by Broadmoor staff, of confusion about the training received to cope with violence within the hospital; in particular the need to develop skills to avert violence before it occurs and the necessity to recognise that conditions of confinement in themselves can lead to violence. It was an unfortunate piece of timing that led the DHSS to follow up the inquest verdict with an announcement on 2nd November, just one month later, that staff at Broadmoor and Rampton were 'pioneering a new method of restraining violent patients'. The 14-day-course devised by the Home Office involves staff learning to immobilise patients while causing minimum physical injury. The precedure apparently involves three people working as a team, with two pinning down a patient by his arms, while the third immobilises the patient's head 'taking care not to damage the neck'.
   . . . It may well be that training in physical restraint is necessary. One of the independent medical witnesses at the Martin inquest suggested as much. What is unacceptable is the impression that the only response to the problem raised by the Martin inquest is refinement in the use of physical force. It is imperative that the independent inquiry into the death of Michael Martin, announced by the DHSS, not only ensures that any techniques of physical restraint are appropriate and used as a last resort, but that the training of staff in how to avoid situations of violence is a central strand of staff training and development. This will involve

examining not only the attitudes of staff but also the nature of special hospitals themselves. It is a complex and controversial issue but its confrontation is something that is owed to both patients and staff.

We fully endorse the view that staff should be trained to avoid situations of violence. Very occasionally, and as a last resort, physical restraining will be necessary although we acknowledge that many people, managers included, feel uncomfortable about the use of physical restraint.

The Bristol survey (Bute, 1979a) produced wide-ranging comments in answer to the question of whether training courses should include lectures on restraint:

'Perhaps it should be included for younger people – they have a need to learn. Perhaps something like judo could be made an option.'

'Yes, I think basic techniques would be useful, especially for residential staff.'

'I don't really know. I suppose there's always the argument that if the social worker comes charging back trying to get somebody into a Half Nelson or something, it's likely to provoke even more anger and violence and create even more problems.'

'No, definitely not!'

'Yes, we should have knowledge of physical holds.'

'No . . . two years' [training] was too short. If something was included on violence something else would have to be missed out.'

One social worker who had been assaulted by a 13 year old boy subsequently received professional advice and supervision from his line manager and yet, in due course, had found himself in a room with the aggressive adolescent coming towards him with a carving knife. This field social worker felt that staff should have some knowledge of physical holds which do not injure the client. Some residential staff have expressed the same view, a point taken up by Liz Ward;

Where talking is insufficient, as when a resident is threatening self-injury, refusing to give up a weapon, or attacking other people, physical restraint may be essential. It may be necessary to use furniture as self protection or for immobilising the violent person. But the physical contact of firm holds is likely to feel more caring.

Holding can be a means of communicating concern as well as establishing control. As the situation loses some of its heat, stroking the head and shoulders or lightly rubbing or massaging the shoulders and back can help dissipate anger and resistance. (Ward, 1984)

Undoubtedly, the use of physical restraint techniques as a method of controlling violence is controversial and very few social services departments appear to condone its use. It is quite clear, however, that physical restraint is used, especially in residential establishments. Leavey in his research in 13 of the 14 community homes run by the London Borough of Hammersmith and Fulham, found that, over the whole 6 months' study period, there were 178 incidents which fell within the definition of violent incident; (the definition was very similar to that used by Belson (1978), except that the psychological dimension used by him was excluded);

> Altogether there were 66 cases of staff being attacked by children. There were 37 other cases where staff had to use 'restraint' to prevent a child hurting itself or someone else. The use of restraining methods by staff also varied strikingly. In three of the busiest homes staff used restraint most frequently; (this primarily took the form of holding or sitting on children). In nine homes, including one busy home, restraint was not used at all. Whether the differences reflect conscious orientation or whether the data is incomplete is an interesting speculation. (Leavey, 1978)

The behaviour problems that face authorities in looking after difficult children have changed very little during the past decade. 267 respondents (79 per cent) in the Wessex study considered that properly taught physical restraint techniques would be beneficial. We suggest that the positive aspects of the procedure should be emphasised in a general context of disturbed client behaviour. The use of restraint should not be seen as a failure of other methods but rather as the application of an appropriate technique to a particular situation. When all is said and done, staff have to face up to the question 'What am I to do when he is coming towards me with a weapon?' Whilst attempts should certainly be made to delay the use of physical restraint, its use will be inevitable in a small minority of instances, and staff will need to be ready to respond responsibly and professionally for the benefit of all who are involved. There will be those who are understandably worried that concern about violence may escalate to a level that is unjustifiable but, equally, others will feel there are dangers in ignoring the problem in the hope that it will go away.

General guidelines

In health establishments, particularly hospitals for the mentally ill or handicapped, as well as group homes, violence arises from time to time and a number of articles have been written in the professional nursing press to help nurses cope with the problem. We noted in Chapter 4 that this is not an issue confined to any one country; Reid (1973) has produced comprehensive guidelines in Canada and Penningroth (1975) produced very useful guidelines in an article written for the 'American Journal of Nursing'. In the United Kingdom, Bowden (1978) has contributed to the discussion and Coffey (1976) produced a helpful survey of nursing literature on the subject. It was in March 1976, however, that the DHSS published Health Circular HC(76)11 on 'The management of violent or potentially violent, hospital patients'. For some time there had been a call for proper guidelines, but the main factor which contributed to the production of guidelines at that time was undoubtedly the Report of the Committee of Inquiry (1975) into the circumstances leading to the death of Mr Daniel Carey at Tooting Bec Hospital on 2 August 1974. The Committee found that staff at the hospital were anxious and uncertain about the management of disturbed patients with a potential for violence.

The Confederation of Health Service Employees (COHSE) whose members were, in the main, employed in hospitals for mental illness or handicap, denounced the 1976 Circular as inadequate and instructed its members to ignore the guidelines. COHSE was concerned that there should be properly laid down guidelines on handling violent patients and, in September 1977 it produced its own booklet which offered information, advice and guidance.

Viewers of the Maybury series on BBC TV may remember an incident where a nurse was suspended on full pay following a violent scuffle with a patient on the psychiatric ward. The words quoted in the subsequent exchange with the union representative were taken from the COHSE guidelines – 'the first thing to do is call for assistance – either verbally or by an agreed warning system. Then: approach the patient and if responsive discuss his or her frustrations and problems . . .' The section on restraining the patient if all else has failed is especially interesting, as several local authority guides fight shy of the area and it can be difficult to get people to commit themselves to comment. It begins by stating that the presence of a few members of staff will often immediately calm the patient. If violence still occurs and restraint is necessary, members are advised to avoid using it in such a way as to provoke more violence, and to use only the minimum degree of force required to control the violence. As for technique:

> clothing rather than limbs should be held to restrain physical activity. If limbs have to be grasped, the following is advised:
> - pinion the patient's arms to his/her side with bear hug from behind and wrestle him or her to the floor;
> - legs and arms should be grasped near the major joints;
> - weight should be placed on the hips and abdomen by lying across the body;
> - if there are attempts at biting, the hair should be grasped firmly and the head held still;
> - if this procedure is followed the possibility of dislocation or fracture will be reduced, and the least long-term discomfort caused;
> - if possible, the patient should than be moved to a quieter environment.
> (COHSE, 1977, p. 22)

The COHSE guidelines were a response to the union's dissatisfaction with the government's circular HC (76) 11, but although there are some differences in the two documents, there are more points of similarity. For example, compare the above passage from the COHSE document with the equivalent section in the appendix to the government circular. (The appendix was prepared by the Royal College of Psychiatrists and the Royal College of Nursing.)

> As a general principle clothing rather than limbs should be held to effect restraint and if limbs have to be grasped they should be held near a major joint in order to reduce the danger of fracture or dislocation. Every effort must be made to safeguard the patient's vulnerable areas, for example, the

neck, throat, chest or abdomen. A patient who has to be restrained should, when possible, not be gripped by the head, throat, or fingers. A bear hug from behind to pinion the arms to the side is valuable and it is better to grip the legs together just above the knees and around the calves rather than separately. If the patient is brought to the ground, he can be very quickly subdued if sufficient members of staff lie with their weight across his legs and trunk and thus immobilise him until further action is decided upon. In exceptional circumstances, as for example, when a patient is biting, the hair may have to be firmly held . . . Should a patient need to be isolated, it should only be for the minimum period necessary until the patient is under control and with the consent of the doctor immediately concerned with the patient's care.

It is recognised that the action suggested for dealing with violent episodes does not cover all eventualities and there will be a need for staff to use considerable initiative in this area. In some instances of extreme violence the degree of force needed becomes a matter of concern for the nurse; it is only possible to reiterate that the degree of force should be the minimum required to control the violence and that it should be applied in a manner calculated to calm rather than to provoke further aggression. It is also recognised that even when all reasonable precautions are taken, physical injury may be caused to the participants in a violent episode. (DHSS, 1976)

The COHSE booklet adopts a crisper style, as can be seen from these extracts. As a whole, it is more detailed and its format makes it less likely to be filed away and forgotten. There are obvious problems, however, in designing guidelines to meet every situation in every setting.

In his study of hospital enquiries John Martin concluded:

This process of developing guidelines has been instructive in that it shows two things: first, that guidelines cannot be all that specific and they have to be interpreted in the light of events; and second, that it is important to consider the implications of violent incidents in terms of having sufficient staff, of providing some training for all grades, of ensuring that regimes are constructive, and of clarifying the responsibilities of all concerned. (Martin, 1984, p. 239)

These themes were picked up in the Wessex study, and any attempt to tackle the problem of violence between clients and staff should explore them together.

Payne and Douglas (1981) identified five key skills which could help turn potentially dangerous situations to good effect.

They were: anticipation (reading what they called 'the social and emotional barometer'); acting decisively and effectively (rather than waiting for the contagious impact on other members of the group); providing 'time out' (to allow isolation from the source of trouble); physical containment (the use of appropriate techniques of restraint); and explicit approach (reinforcing non-violent actions, monitoring violence and developing targets for change). They advocated programmes of training to try to develop these skills.

Many staff would feel uncomfortable using restraint, but the issue is not one to be sidestepped. Several health authorities have now produced their own guidelines for members of staff, in which it is accepted that it will be necessary to exercise physical control when a person makes an attack on someone else, or when a person becomes disturbed to the extent that there is a danger of injury to self and/or others. In Southampton, for example, the Royal South Hants Hospital managers have formulated a security policy document which includes guidelines for staff on avoiding and dealing with incidents of violence. Extensive consultations took place within the hospital before the procedures were adopted.

Legal guidelines

Whilst it is relatively easy, after the event, to decide whether and how intervention should have been made, it became quite clear from the Bristol survey that many members of staff are unsure of their rights in respect of the law on self defence (Bute, 1979a). The use of violence to repel violence is, in law, perfectly acceptable, subject to one qualification, which is that it must only entail reasonable force. What the law allows is the use of reasonable force either to prevent the committing of a crime or to apprehend the criminal. All departmental guidelines should include information about the legal boundaries when dealing with an assault. The following extract is from Hampshire's booklet on the subject;

> Violence occasionally occurs very suddenly and, at such times, there is usually no opportunity to call for assistance from the police. The use of

physical restraint to repel violence is, in law, perfectly acceptable, subject to the qualification that the restraint must only entail reasonable force. 'Reasonable' means that amount of force which is sufficient to stop the attacker or to prevent yourself being injured. It should not be greater. Courts will expect you to retreat whenever possible and if the choice is between hitting your attacker or running away then you should take the latter course of action. There will be very few occasions when the only way in which you can protect yourself is by harming the person but, if this is necessary, it is all right in law. Whenever possible get away and try to get assistance. It is better to overpower an attacker than to inflict injury. Better still to simply get away although there will be times when this would be an unacceptable course of action. Your assistance might be needed immediately, for example, by other people who are being threatened, or the assailant might be intent on harming himself.

If you have used physical restraint to the extent that the person has been forced to the ground, it is important not to overreact by using more force than is necessary to keep him there. As soon as sufficient help arrives, relax holds and attempt to gain control by talking rather than by using physical means. (Bute, 1980)

Practical dilemmas

Only in very extreme situations, when there is clearly no alternative, should staff call for assistance from other people who may happen to be present during an attack. Visitors to an area office, or residents in a home, or trainees in a day centre may have a role to play in calling other staff to assist. If at all possible their role should be restricted to such passive activity. This not only ensures that confusion of roles is avoided but it also prevents complications arising in respect of legal confrontation or insurance claims. Where it is obvious that active assistance is immediately required and would prevent a deterioration in the situation, then the involvement of other people is justifiable.

We acknowledge that occasionally violent outbursts may be caused by staff members who, by attitude or action, precipitate an incident. Payne and Douglas (1981) suggest there is little doubt that some adults command respect by their presence 'but children will never "try it on" when "so and so" is on duty'. It is also clear that some children feel more secure with some adults than others: '. . . children are very adept at exploiting what they perceive are adults' strengths and weaknesses, tolerance thresholds, whether high or low, and whether there are positive and negative consequences from co-operating with them'. These experienced residential care staff also accept that, very occasionally, physical restraint will be necessary;

> Clumsy handling often increases the problem, making the regaining of self control, which should always be the objective of intervention, more difficult. In using restraint, staff must use their understanding of the child; although some children may respond positively to physical closeness, others may resent and fear it, and in these cases may reinforce the violent behaviour and loss of identity.

Whether or not physical restraint has been used, it will be necessary for staff involved in a violent incident to have opportunity to discuss it in detail with the line manager. This, in itself, should be very supportive and will provide an opportunity to decide how best to proceed with the problem. Injuries may require medical attention; in the absence of internal injuries, some liquid refreshment will help in the overall treatment for shock, the extent of which should never be underestimated. In extreme cases, it might be appropriate simply to encourage the victim to spend time in a horizontal position in a rest room. A companion should remain in order to reassure, comfort, and provide support and a listening ear for when the victim is ready to talk.

Depending upon the nature and circumstances of the assault, one of the decisions which has to be made at quite an early stage is whether or not to involve the police. This is necessary not only because of the requirements of the Criminal Injuries Compensation Board, but also because the acts of many violent offenders are best dealt with by the judicial processes. The line manager will be in a good position to discuss referral to the police; in fact it will sometimes be necessary for that decision to be made independently. Understandably, the police appreciate early referral and this is not always possible in departments where staff may be unaware whether there is a departmental policy and, if so, what it is. Managers should be very clear regarding the responsibility for deciding whether or not to prosecute. In general, it would appear that the decision is best made in the work place. In many cases, the police will have been already called to assist in resolving the conflict. It will still be necessary to decide whether or not to proceed with prosecution.

In the large majority of serious cases it will be in the longer term interests of the assailant as well as the victim, the agency and other staff members, if prosecution is made. Occasionally, victims of assault will need opportunity to discuss this aspect at some length because of the feeling of guilt which can be roused, and the possible reversal of roles in causing a client to be taken to court. It should also be remembered that some people are best helped by ensuring that they are aware that certain behaviour will not be tolerated under any circumstances. Imposed sanctions sometimes help to produce a sense of security for people who would otherwise experience difficulty in controlling their aggressive urges.

Reporting and recording

An incident of violence should always be reported and recorded in detail, as soon after the occurrence as possible. Millham *et al.* (1976) referred to the tendency of staff to filter the truth from a report of an incident in order to achieve an objective. For example, certain aspects of a resident's behaviour would be emphasised if an attempt was being made to get the boy transferred to another establishment. Similarly one suspects that many staff in the personal social services will record in a file in such a way as to protect themselves. In so doing, there may well be a filtering of the truth, for whatever reason. The greater the delay in reporting, the more likely this is to happen. Details are omitted or changed in emphasis as a result of selective memory processes and the constraints of ego defence mechanisms.

It would appear that very few local authorities have special forms for reporting incidents of violence, and this is understandable considering the difficulties of deciding what constitutes a violent act. Normally, it is expected that a report would be included in the statutory book for recording accidents and, if the incident warranted such, a verbal report would be made to the line manager. In the Bristol survey (Bute, 1979a) the local social services department appeared to have no established criteria for reporting; (this refers to the county where the study was carried out, and not to Avon Social Services). There was an expectation that residential and day care staff would record such events in the home's diary; similarly, fieldworkers were expected to include details in the client's case record.

Are there any benefits to be gained by the use of specific report forms? Under the scheme administered for the Home Office by the Criminal Injuries Compensation Board, the victim of a crime of violence can obtain compensation from the Board . Normally, one of the conditions of an award is that the incident giving rise to the injury has been reported to the police without delay, although not necessarily by the victim. In the past, in the case of incidents occurring in hospitals, particularly when the aggressor has been a mentally disordered patient and the victim a member of the hospital staff, such a report has not always been made. Consequently, injured persons applying to the Criminal Injuries Compensation Board have, on occasion, either been refused compensation or, at best, obtained an award only on appeal;

Even when the circumstances of a particular incident are fully known and disclose no blameworthy conduct on the part of an applicant, the Board will only rarely excuse an applicant's failure in his obvious duty to report crimes of violence to the police with a view to bringing the offender to justice; where, however, the circumstances surrounding the incident are obscure for one reason or another and the applicant's testimony is unsupported by any independent evidence, the importance of an early report to the police so that they can carry out immediate enquiries into the background becomes crucial. Irrespective of the provisions of the Scheme, it is essential, if the rising tide of crime is to be stemmed, that all victims of crime should, without delay, report the circumstances of the incident or their injury to the police and thereafter co-operate fully with the police in their enquiries. (CICB, 1983)

It would therefore seem important for staff to make a comprehensive departmental report of any assault and, in the absence of an authoritative guideline, to make a second report to the police in order to cover the possibility of a subsequent claim for compensation. A second reason for writing a specific departmental report would be to assist in the collating of relevant information. The absence of recorded information has hampered the task of obtaining a clear indication of the extent and nature of the problem of violence towards staff. Finally, of course, it is good professional practice to make a proper recording of such incidents in case files.

Conclusions

What to do in the event of violence arising is a question that has been posed many times, but has apparently provoked few answers, if the professional social work press is anything to judge by. During the course of a career, most staff will experience violence or the threat of such, and in this chapter we have sought to explore ways in which it can be handled effectively.

We have not tried to produce a step-by-step (or blow-by-blow) account of what to do, because violence arises in so many different ways and thus defies systematic approaches to the problem. Instead, we have sought to raise the questions that usually surface whenever the topic is discussed. Should physical restraint be used and, if so, to what extent and how? Could a person be prosecuted if, in using physical restraint techniques, they injure the assailant? Can we learn from the experience of other professions, and perhaps of other countries? Are there staff members who sometimes precipitate violence? Should the police be involved in prosecution as well as helping to deal with the actual incident? What else can be and should be done after the incident? This final question is sufficiently important for us to consider in greater depth in the next chapter.

Points for practice

- When violence is threatened, it is important that staff should make every effort to keep control of the situation.
- First of all, assistance from other staff should be called for.
- Secondly, an attempt should be made to discuss with the violent person his or her frustrations and problems.

- If all else fails, physical restraint may help to control violence, but with the employment of minimum force.
- The use of physical restraint in social work is controversial.
- Guidelines, such as those produced by the DHSS and COHSE, may provide useful advice about techniques of restraint.
- It is usually better to retreat and get away if possible.
- The involvement of persons other than staff should be avoided whenever possible.
- Staff involved in violent incidents should always have the opportunity to discuss what has happened in detail with the line manager and with colleagues.
- The extent of shock should not be underestimated.
- The questions of police involvement and prosecution should be given early consideration by the line manager.
- Violent incidents should be reported and recorded at the first opportuinity.
- Victims may be eligible for compensation from the CICB, as long as the incident has been reported to the police.

6

What Support Should I Expect?

No matter how the incident happened, victims of an assault almost invariably have to come to terms with subsequent feelings of guilt. The reactions of peers, supervisors and management staff can be quite crucial at such times. 'Fortunately, my superiors and colleagues could not have been more kind and my self-critical feelings did not last long' said Dennis Powell (1983), whilst Dr Frank Wells appreciated the physical presence of others even if, seemingly, they were able to do very little to assist in a practical way;

> At times of adversity you discover who are your friends, and the enormous number of visitors I actually received or who were apparently precluded from coming in was very gratifying and indeed satisfying, out of all proportion to the relatively trivial injury I believe I had had. The early arrival of the vicar had genuinely caused me some concern, but he proved to be a great friend, not a prophet of doom. (Wells, 1983)

Dr Wells was eased back into full-time general practice by his understanding partners after recuperating for two weeks, although he was not allowed to drive for six weeks. Sally Green expressed appreciation for the support she received from her principal area officer, who did a lot to reassure her that she was not to blame, that the incident could not have been avoided and that she could not have been expected to react differently. Several months later, however, she was still wondering whether this was, in fact, the case (Green, 1982).

Guilt reactions can present themselves in a variety of guises, ranging from the straightforward 'Could I have avoided it?' 'Should I have done anything different?' to the more explicit 'Was it my fault?' (Green, 1982). Much will depend upon the circumstances and subsequent experience of the individual concerned. The ordeal can continue for a lengthy period of time, especially if the matter is subsequently taken to Court.

A young woman assistant who was nearly raped . . . was extremely courageous and did not take any time off but management felt she should be relieved of being on duty on her own for a while and we tried to give her sympathy and support. She was most apprehensive of resuming night duty on her own again but what she most hated was the court appearances, and having to give evidence. The police were very pleasant to her and the court was sympathetic but *she* felt on trial, and feared that they may secretly be thinking that 'she asked for it'. (Powell, 1983)

Dennis Powell illustrates his own experience in a slightly different way.

At that time I was reading an American book called *The Onion Field*, based on a true story, it tells of two police officers who stopped a couple of small time criminals in a car and were disarmed and taken prisoner. After being driven around, one officer was shot and killed and the other escaped. The survivor suffered terribly from self-recrimination made worse by unsympathetic superiors and colleagues. Like him, I too felt self-critical, despising myself for not being more skilful, resourceful and brave. The people we see in fictional violence on film and television conduct themselves so well, apparently without fear and they always seem to be rewarded with ultimate success. Compared with the standards they set, real life victims can only feel inferior. (Powell, 1983)

The General Practitioner who had been assaulted expressed his feelings of guilt in a slightly different way:

I certainly slept a lot during the succeeding 48 hours, something which surprised my consultant, who always gave me the impression, though he never said so, that I had overreacted to the attack and was making the most of it. Eight years later that impression remains, although the care I had was of the highest standard. (Wells, 1983)

This sense of guilt, together with the need for support, should not be underestimated or taken lightly.

Professional peers and immediate managers will have a very

important role to play in providing an opportunity to talk about what happened. During the hours immediately following an assault, the short term objective of this support should be to provide opportunities for victims to verbalise their fears in order to work through any guilt feelings. Some people also find it helpful to write comprehensive notes about the event. In the previous chapter we commented on the importance of making detailed notes as soon as practicable; whilst this helps to provide an accurate recording of the event, it should also be encouraged because it often enables individuals to get things into perspective. In all work centres, post incident discussion should focus upon how the incident was handled – method, techniques, what worked, what didn't and why – so that teaching programmes can be reinforced at the time of, or soon after, the crisis.

Coping with fear and guilt

Most of those who have experienced a violent attack – or even the threat of one – will agree that it can be extremely frightening. This was pointed out by a field social worker who had been threatened with murder:

> I think, while the actual threats were being hurled at me, I felt very nervous. I was nervous anyway, because I had an idea that there could be some trouble in the court, and I always tend to feel very nervous when going to court and very unhappy with the verbal statement requesting a place of safety order; but in a sense, when it was happening I couldn't believe what I was hearing, and then I think I was so shocked when they ordered Mr O's arrest, because I think I had heard this sort of thing from him before – perhaps not quite so bad – but I wasn't expecting them to arrest him, so it was a very mixed confusion really and I was very worried.
>
> I think I'd have been a lot more frightened had I been in the situation on my own. Obviously with two magistrates and policemen and a court full of people, I wasn't as frightened at that point for my safety as I might have been had I been in the house visiting. When I came back to the office, I think I then felt very shaken, and I felt worried that he was on remand and likely to go to prison. I felt concerned about that. I also felt worried that if he wasn't in prison, I might be at risk, so I felt a bit guilty, in a sense that I wanted him locked up, because I think it's against a social worker's nature

to want her client locked up, but I felt quite guilty that I wanted it and quite glad that he probably was going to be.

Colleagues in the office were very supportive, but I didn't feel I could function particularly well for the rest of that day.

During the 24 hours following the court incident I found myself looking around a bit and wondering if any of his friends were around, because of the threats that Mrs O had made, but I think that's diminished quite a lot now. (Bute, 1979b)

In the days immediately following an assault, as well as in the period following associated court proceedings, these mixed feelings of guilt and fright will come very much to the fore. For some people, the experience itself can be thoroughly disabling, and practical support from colleagues will be essential. It can be very reassuring, for example, to be offered an escort from the office to the car park, even though the chance of further assault from 'accomplices' may be highly unlikely. Workload will need careful supervision until problems arising from the assault have been worked through; discussion should take place about future agency policy for working with the client in question, and this should include professional issues as well as management's response. Whilst in some cases it will be important for the same member of staff to remain directly involved, in others it will be necessary to change the worker or, at least, share the responsibility with another colleague. Visiting and interviewing in pairs can be considered and, in exceptional cases, senior management might want to take the unusual step of writing to the aggressor to say that violence will not be tolerated and visits to offices must be by appointment. Those attending day centres, as well as people living in residential homes or hostels, may need to be written to in similar terms. Whilst some Directors are likely to view such procedures as unnecessarily authoritarian, others will readily acknowledge the importance of being seen to support their staff. In addition, it should be remembered that some individuals positively benefit from controls that stem from proscriptive action, and it could be very much in such a person's best long term interests to receive a letter from 'Authority'. It is well known that some acutely violent people are afraid of their own violent urges, and seek controls over their aggression.

The role of managers

Not all staff have the advantage of good support from senior managers. Instructive comparisons can be made between violence in social work agencies and extreme indiscipline in schools. Comber and Whitfield have provided a number of illustrations from their research into indiscipline:

> The following incident occurred with a class of thirty first year pupils in a large, urban boys secondary school.
> A general science lesson on acids and alkalis was being taken in an ordinary classroom in a separate building that housed the first and second year classes some considerable distance from the main school building. There was no science laboratory and a meagre quantity of materials and apparatus was kept in a store room not directly connected to the classroom. The master had improvised a demonstration table and had prepared a demonstration lesson with materials carried in from the store.
> The lesson went well for about an hour when one boy began to make a nuisance of himself and was soon joined by two more. These boys took bottles of acid from the demonstration table and threatened to throw them over the teacher. When the teacher tried to take the bottles from the boys, three more boys joined in and a chair was thrown at the teacher as he struggled with them. The teacher was cut off from any help and the lesson ended in pandemonium. (Comber and Whitfield, 1979, p. 25)

It is important to note the authors' claim that, in these very difficult situations, teachers often find themselves unsupported by senior colleagues.

> . . . Heads are not perceived by many teachers as giving a sufficiently strong lead against indiscipline in their schools [and are] afraid of the reaction of . . . [the] local Education Authority or, even more frequently, apparently unaware that a problem of indiscipline exists in their school. (Comber and Whitfield, 1979, p. 8)

If heads are unaware, then the hierarchy of local education authorities will also be unaware and this, perhaps, goes some way to explaining why in the Bristol survey a request to a small number of education authorities for information in respect of training and departmental guidelines on coping with aggression drew an almost complete blank (Bute, 1979a). One authority responded rather vaguely '. . . the only advice given appears to be from the Headteachers Association which is simply "if difficulties arise, call the Police",' whilst another indicated that 'the advice of this Authority to staff in schools and Education Welfare Officers is that, in appropriate cases, they should take private legal action against members of the public who are violent towards them'.

Another replied: 'No training is arranged for staff, teaching or non-teaching, and no specific advice is given. Generally speaking, one would hope that staff were capable of avoiding violent confrontations.'

A further reply stated that 'This Authority gives virtually no formal guidance to staff in schools or Education Welfare Officers in dealing with violent clients. The only instruction which is handed out is a rather cautionary document on the use of corporal punishment in schools.'

That might appear to be somewhat unhelpful, but imagine how unsupported a head teacher might feel if he worked for the county education officer who replied in the following terms:

> Obviously all staff have a duty under the Health and Safety at Work Act to act as far as is reasonably practical in a way that does not endanger themselves or others and staff are not, therefore, asked to enter unnecessarily hazardous situations . . . when asked for advice, we would always reiterate the Act's wording that staff should take all care that is reasonably practicable.

Managers of staff in many social work agencies have similarly failed to provide guidance for staff who are vulnerable, because they work in situations where they are involved with violent or potentially violent people. It should be remembered that support can be given in many forms and, if given in the right way at the appropriate time, might well be a contribution to the prevention of violence. Many managers have, quite rightly, responded to pressures to ensure that comprehensive guidelines are available for staff working with parents whose children have suffered from non-accidental injury. Regretfully, guidelines are not usually so clear – and in many departments do not exist – in relation to the prevention and management of violence towards staff. There may be a few directors of social services who still take the view that 'Most members of staff accept that the threat of violence is part of the job' (Fry, 1983) and offer no more than this bald statement, as if washing their hands of any subsequent violence. Other departments have demonstrated a desire to be seen as supportive. The local authority's solicitor in Birmingham, for example, has apparently agreed to act on behalf of Social Services Department staff who are attacked at work (Fry, 1983). In the Bristol survey, enquiries to a small number of social services departments revealed a genuine concern for what appeared to be a growing problem, although it was acknowledged on more than one occasion that no reliable statistics of assault were available except by manual extraction from accident report books; guidelines to staff for coping with the problem were generally considered a good idea, but very few authorities had produced anything in print (Bute, 1979a). Northampton and Hampshire Social Services Departments had produced documents in draft form at that stage. Since that time, a number of local authorities have purchased copies of Hampshire's guidelines to staff, and some have written to request formal permission to adapt them for use in their local situations.

In the health sector, guidelines have been available in several health authorities for a number of years. COHSE's report for its members was published in September 1977, and some health authorities followed the example of the Maudsley Hospital staff who produced guidelines which were brief but to the point. Several departments, like the West Midlands Regional Health Authority, produced comprehensive policy documents whilst, at the same time publishing a much smaller outline to serve as an *aide-mémoire* for staff involved in violent incidents.

Trade unions and professional organisations

The British Association of Social Workers (BASW), National Association of Local Government Officers (NALGO), National Association of Probation Officers (NAPO), and Social Care Association (SCA) all show some interest in the problem of violence, but to our knowledge none of these organisations maintains comprehensive records of violence towards staff;

From a sample of serious incidents reported to NALGO's legal department in the period 1976–81, researcher Anne Greaves found half involved staff employed by SSDs. The great majority of these assaults were by young people, the majority of them in residential homes, and they involved a fearsome range of weapons – including a wrought iron plant stand, a car, scissors and knives. They testify to the extreme aggression social workers occasionally have to face . . .

When NALGO sent a questionnaire to all local government branches requesting details of assaults on members in 1979 and 1980, it found that it was impossible to get a complete picture of the problem, which seemed to vary from one incident in two years to one a week.

BASW and the RCA also receive reports of incidents and have taken action to help their members gain compensation for injuries. But there again, there is no suggestion they hear about anything other than the minority of cases. (Crine, 1982)

From our own direct enquiries of these organisations, we established that BASW would give full legal advice and assistance to its members through its advice and representation fund: there would also be the possibility of providing the services of a solicitor or barrister in any subsequent court case. The advice given to its members by the SCA usually takes the form of advising on civil rights in law, in addition to discussion of the professional practice events surrounding the incident.

Statistics

While some support can be provided by standard guidelines, and more practical support can be given at the time of or immediately following a violent incident, other support will be ongoing and its immediate benefits may not be so obvious. For example, staff are often encouraged and reassured when they know that their senior managers acknowledge the problem and are prepared to do something about it. This acknowledgement might take the form of collating statistical information, to help gauge the extent of the problem. It will also be evident in staff training programmes.

We acknowledge that meaningful statistics are very difficult to obtain because of differing perceptions of violence, a point brought out very well in Belson's researches (1978) as well as in work carried out by Millham, Bullock and Hosie (1978). The

Dartington team has questioned the reliability of evidence gained form residential establishments. This is not because material is suppressed or unavailable;

> On the contrary violent incidents, when they occur, are reported at length to case conferences or in boys' records. However, such accounts are not written with research in mind; thus the actual details of any violent incident become difficult to unravel . . . There were several schools in our research where staff frequently hit children and where the formal punishment records underestimated the number of violent incidents that occurred, but which, nevertheless, were quite happy with their levels of violence. No one seemed particularly anxious in this rumbustious environment, except possibly a visitor, and in such schools violence was not defined as a problem. In contrast in several cosy family group homes for younger children, where staff were particularly sensitive to boys' needs, violent behaviour was often viewed as a major concern. Staff complained that children swore, that they hit each other, that they damaged property or were noisy and defiant. In contrast, staff perspectives in more permissive regimes are quite different. In such contexts, violence is frequently defined as acting-out behaviour, and aggressive attacks on staff, even physical attacks, are viewed as valuable crisis moments for exploration and resolution. In such contexts, violence is written about and perceived in a way that is very different from those found in more rigid regimes such as those for boys of senior age. Thus, with all these real problems in the way of any investigation into violence among adolescents in residential schools, it is not surprising that so little empirical research has been undertaken.

For these reasons, it is very difficult, and usually unwise, to attach considerable significance to statistical information on violence. In some situations there will be a gross underestimation of violent incidents towards staff. It is obviously important to establish the context of the group being studied. At a simple level, trends can then be identified which will sometimes be helpful in obtaining additional resources such as improved facilities, more staff and training programmes, and may additionally provide valuable information about the nature and extent of violence in particular establishments.

The Health Service Advisory Committee's working party which investigated the problem of violence in the National Health Service decided to recommend that a questionnaire be sent out to one in ten of all NHS staff working in six health authorities. Previous evidence, mainly anecdotal, had indicated that physical assaults on general practitioners were running at about fifty each year and increasing (Pulse, 1984). The findings of the questionnaire have yet to be published.

Although it is difficult to quantify violence, it is clear that staff who work in residential homes, day care establishments and social work offices are occasionally confronted by aggressive and violent people. Staff who work in centres where violence is a problem – or a potential problem – will need to develop special expertise in coping with physical assault. The organisation of training programmes which concentrate on the prevention of violence, and passive techniques for physical restraint, is one way in which managers can demonstrate positive support for their staff. Training implications will be dealt with more fully in Chapter 8.

External help

Sometimes, it is possible for external organisations and individuals to provide appropriate support. This help might be practical, for example financial assistance from the Criminal Injuries Compensation Board; at other times, members of trade unions and professional organisations will seek professional and legal advice or representation. In some parts of the country, excellent work is undertaken by volunteers working with victims' support schemes. These schemes attempt to provide advice and a listening ear for victims of crime, including violent acts, as soon as possible after the incident has occurred. Their assistance is also very practical, and may consist of putting victims in touch with other agencies which may be able to help (such as the Criminal Injuries Compensation Board), as well as helping with insurance claims against personal injury, theft or loss of property. Volunteers are usually trained and often have wide experience of giving all sorts of help and advice. Details of existing local victims' support schemes are available from local police officers.

Legal and financial help

In consequence of the Health and Safety at Work legislation, employers are required to recognise and accept responsibility for providing a safe and healthy workplace. Under the 1974 Act, all employees have a duty to take reasonable care for their own health and safety and for those other persons who may be affected by their actions. Personal accident insurance cover is usually arranged by local authorities, and this enables them to meet losses and liabilities as and when they arise. As a result, various benefits are usually payable to an employee of an authority in respect of death or injury sustained whilst on duty.

In addition, any aggrieved person is able to apply to the Criminal Injuries Compensation Board, which administers a scheme for compensating victims of crimes of violence (see Appendix). Table 5.1 illustrates the number of applications received over the past five years.

Table 5.1 *Number of applications to CICB 1979–84*

	England & Wales	Scotland	Total
1979–80	18,948	3,853	22,801
1980–1	20,613	4,066	24,679
1981–2	22,099	4,416	26,515
1982–3	24,635	4,805	29,440
1983–4	26,828	5,111	31,939

Source: CICB 1984

Table 5.2 *Percentage increase in number of applicants (Comparison with previous year)*

	England & Wales	Scotland	Total
1979–80	+ 4.8%	− 0.7%	+ 3.8%
1980–1	+ 8.8%	+ 5.5%	+ 8.2%
1981–2	+ 7.2%	+ 8.6%	+ 7.4%
1982–3	+11.5%	+ 8.8%	+11.0%
1983–4	+ 8.9%	+ 6.4%	+ 8.5%

Source: CICB 1984

Table 5.3 *Total compensation paid 1980-4*

	1980-1 £	1981-2 £	1982-3 £	1983-4 £
England & Wales	18,288,242	18,085,617	24,616,030	27,161,359
Scotland	3,174,222	3,891,079	4,828,645	5,659,413
Total	21,462,464	21,976,695	29,444,675	32,820,772

Source: CICB 1984

The percentage increase in the number of applicants each year over the past five years is shown in Table 5.2. The total compensation paid during the past four years is indicated in Table 5.3. The sum of £32 820 772 paid in 1983-4 represents an increase of 53 per cent over 1980-1.

Crimes of violence (paragraph 4 of the Scheme) can be interpreted in various ways and, for those who are employed by departments of social services, the following illustration of a home help claimant is worthy of note:

A home help was going to the house of one of her elderly clients and as she pushed the garden gate open her hand stuck to it. The whole top surface had been liberally and deliberately coated with superglue. The person or persons responsible were never identified. She was cut free by the Fire Brigade and taken to hospital where the remnants of the gate were removed with solvents. The case was referred for hearing by the Single Member. After hearing evidence a hearing Board decided that the application fell within the scope of the Scheme; because the injuries had not resolved and the applicant was still being treated as a hospital outpatient, an interim award of £250 was made. (CICB, 1983)

Conclusions

Acts of violence must always be dealt with professionally and competently. Whilst local authorities should not seek to condone or defend actions by staff that it judges to be wrong or inappropriate, equally, there should be no blame attached to a staff member who has acted in good faith and consistently with any training he has received. Unfortunately, our experience and our enquiries have shown that few departments are aware of the extent of the problem, and even those who are may not acknowledge it as an issue that requires intervention from management. Educational establishments and operational units seldom provide comprehensive training or guidelines despite the fact that violence and the threat of violence can be very frightening and even disabling, as we have shown in this chapter. The common reaction of guilt, whether or not justified, creates an essential need for peers, supervisors and senior managers to give active and sympathetic support to the assaulted person. Surprisingly, such support cannot be taken for granted. Comparative examples provided by county education officers demonstrate a certain amount of denial that the problem exists. We readily acknowledge that serious violence is not a frequent occurrence, but staff who do experience it will feel much more supported if the issues of statistical collation, management guidelines and training programmes have been thought through and acted upon. Finally, we have considered briefly the role of trade unions and professional organisations, as well as the more practical financial support which is available from local authority personal accident insurance covers and the Criminal Injuries Compensation Board.

Points for practice

- Feelings of guilt and fear in the victims of assault may be long-lasting, and need to be treated sensitively.
- Victims should have immediate and extensive opportunities to talk about their feelings and about the assault, with colleagues and managers.
- Discussing what has happened should also help staff to learn about the handling of future incidents.
- Victims should be offered every practical support.
- The future management of the assailant should be planned; exceptional firmness may be appropriate.
- Management should provide staff with clear guidelines.

- Management should recognise the importance of supportive action.
- Senior managers should inform themselves of the extent of violent incidents and arrange relevant training programmes.
- The especial risks to staff in some work settings should be acknowledged.
- Trades Unions and Professional Associations may be able to provide legal assistance for their members.
- Victims' support schemes may provide practical help and advice.
- Staff may be able to make personal accident claims against their employers' insurance cover.
- Staff may also be able to obtain compensation from the Criminal Injuries Compensation Board.

7

Organising to Reduce Risk

It is instructive to study the 'Points for Practice', which conclude the past four chapters, from the perspective of the manager. Many, if not most of the issues raised have immediate and practical implications for those who organise fieldwork, residential and day care services. The purpose of this chapter is to emphasise and clarify the significance of management and planning in the prevention of violence towards staff.

Staffing issues

In Chapter 4 we noted the importance of taking care to appoint the kind of staff who are unlikely to provoke violence. It is equally important to take account of the personalities of staff already in post. It is not safe to make an assumption that experienced staff are always well equipped to cope with violence. They may well be hard working, trained, administratively efficient and genuinely concerned for residents but still lacking in certain qualities needed in a particular home. This was the conclusion reached by Oxfordshire's social services committee in the case of Frederick Bolter, who was the warden of Orchard House, near Oxford. In 1973 he was convicted of causing one resident grievous bodily harm and of four other charges of assault on other residents. The home was for elderly mentally infirm people.

The case was considered by Paul Harrison who noted that

as the senior probation officer reported to the trial court, he was a man of singular integrity, but excessive zeal, expecting everything he required to be accepted without question. As a result, staff found him difficult to work with. Bolter seems to have worked excessive hours, rarely taking the leave due to him. But his methods of communicating to, re-training and controlling the residents were 'far too disciplinarian' and his use of physical control was 'wholly unjustifiable'. Even here, the [social services committee] report accepts that Bolter was not a sadist, but really believed he was acting in the best interests of the residents. (Harrison, 1974, p. 250)

Harrison examined the responsibilities of the social services department in the appointment (by the department's predecessors) of Bolter, and in allowing him to remain there for so long. He concluded that the original appointment in 1964 seemed sound and that the response to complaints had been reasonable. Harrison also considered the difficulties of working with residents who were occasionally violent and frequently difficult in their behaviour. The issue was clearly put by the new warden, James Widon:

If they go for you, you have somehow to restrain them without giving a blow yourself . . . But if you hold them on the wrist their skin is so fragile that the next day they may be covered in bruises. A situation like the one that arose at Orchard House makes all residential workers terribly conscious of the dangers. If someone falls out of bed at night, our first thought is what will this look like to the relatives? If you don't do the right thing, society is ready to throw the book at you. (Harrison, 1974, p. 251)

Harrison concluded with a description of the home as it was in 1974, with a lack of resources and a lack of real participation by the residents in deciding how to spend their days. This led to some scathing final comments as Harrison wondered

what kind of a society it is that hives off its old people and will not provide the resources to make their last years worth living; that pays miserably those who have assumed the burden on our behalf, but punishes them mercilessly if they fail even for a moment in that humanity we ourselves seem to lack. Frederick Bolter is a victim of that hypocrisy. (Harrison, 1974, p. 252)

Payne and Douglas (1981) considered that some thought should be given, when organising rotas in residential care, as to which combinations of staff would minimise violence. Such planning may well be sensible but it can clearly only be achieved when levels of staffing and resources make it possible.

The working environment

Managers are responsible for the surroundings in which staff work. This is recognised in a recent psychiatric text which provides interesting comparisons with social work. After a brief but useful examination of the relationship between psychiatric disorder and crime, Taylor summarises some of the key points in managing the potentially violent patient in a hospital setting:

> Potentially violent patients should only be seen or nursed in areas where clear observation is possible, to which other staff have rapid and easy access and where an alarm system is readily available. Obvious makeshift weapons such as heavy ashtrays must not be lying around . . . If reassurance is failing, withdrawal is better than confrontations. It is vital, for example, not to get into a conflict over trying to remove a weapon. Physical restraint may become necessary but should only be initiated when several members of staff are available. (Taylor, 1983, p. 144)

These points may have application in other settings, and are especially relevant to hospital based social workers as Taylor makes the point that all staff in the hospital should know the policy on management of violence. Taylor's comments echo our earlier observations that alarm systems are essential and that potential weapons should not be left lying around, as well as pointing managers towards a careful consideration of the physical setting in which people are placed. Taylor's remarks about hospitals are clearly relevant to day care and residential settings in social work, and in the same context we have already noted the need to review reception and interviewing facilities in fieldwork agencies.

Risk reduction in different settings

The general objective of managers should be to create a climate in which both staff and the people they serve will feel secure. That in itself will do much to minimise the risk of aggressive behaviour. It can be achieved in practice by the maintenance of an appropriate working ethos in all settings, by systematic and thorough recording procedures, by careful allocation and management of people thought to be potentially violent, and by giving particular attention to the known 'high-risk' situations in which people are deprived of their liberty – 'Place of Safety' orders, hospital admissions and occasionally the placing of elderly people in Part III accommodation.

Residential work

Violence as one of the risks faced by social workers in the process of admission to residential care was analysed by Brearley *et al.* (1980), and violence within residential care itself was looked at by Walton and Elliott (1980). In both books it was acknowledged that risk occasionally must be faced, or its level increased to meet other more important requirements. This is the dilemma all social workers have to face, and although working towards a regime with increased benefits for the welfare of the residents may often reduce the level of violence towards staff, this will not always be so. It will be much more likely to reduce the risk than to remove it. Achieving a good balance in the relationship between the two will usually necessitate full discussion. Two complicating factors which should also be considered in any such analysis are that firstly, staff expectations of behaviour will affect their reporting of incidents, and secondly the related level of violence from staff to residents is likely to be under-reported.

As we have noted in Chapter 4, there is considerable evidence from the psychiatric field that a change towards more therapeutic community ideals can reduce significantly the level of violence in wards. To some extent these findings can be translated into the equivalent local authority residential forms of care. In recent years similar themes have emerged in studies of children in local authority care. Millham *et al.* challenged the traditional belief that disruptive behaviour was inherent in the child. In their study of a range of secure accommodation for children, they concluded that the way establishments were managed had a considerable effect on the level of violence. They suggest that the change to more relaxed regimes in four community homes with education (CHEs) contributed to an increase in the level of violence. However, they regarded the level as still being low. For example:

> In a three-year period, 1972–4, boys hit staff on only eleven occasions. In those three years, nearly 220 boys will have been in the school, so the frequency of assaults on staff works out at one incident in every three months. This pattern is repeated in the other schools and hardly corroborates popular ideas of a surging tide of violence in residential establishments. (Millham *et al.*, 1978, p. 61)

They were not suggesting that moves towards more psychotherapeutic regimes were in any way wrong, but only that in the context of the aims of CHEs and who was using them, one result was a rise in the level of aggression

Some of the increase in violence was attributed to the closer relationships between staff and boys resulting from the change in regime. They also considered that most of the violent incidents were avoidable, but that very few of the staff had received any instruction on how to prevent such incidents. They found some encouragement in the fact that most adolescent violence was logical. If it is a response to demanding social situations rather than an uncontrolled drive, then youthful aggression can be checked and confrontation can be manipulated by adults (Millham *et al.*, 1978, p. 66).

We have concentrated so far mainly on individual incidents of violence. Those interested in factors leading to riots in residential establishments might benefit from consideration of the work of Clarke and Sinclair (1970), who identified a range of relevant factors, including the admission of new residents and the lack of communication between staff and residents.

Day centres

Day centres are a relatively recent development in social work in this country, and so there is much less literature about them than is the case in residential work. The most comprehensive examination of day centres to date has been the five year national survey undertaken by the National Institute for Social

Work (Carter, 1981). Apart from day nurseries and other facilities for children, most of the facilities provided by public or voluntary agencies in day hospitals or day centres were considered, in a survey which covered thirteen areas of England and Wales selected at random.

Centres were grouped into categories, and the percentage of units for each user group was estimated as follows:

> 39 per cent were for elderly people
> 19 per cent were for mentally handicapped adults
> 19 per cent were for physically handicapped adults
> 14 per cent were for mentally ill adults
> 4 per cent were for elderly, confused people
> 2 per cent were for families
> 2 per cent were mixed
> 1 per cent were for adult offenders

This part of the survey was carried out in 1976. No facilities were found for drug addicts, homeless people or young people, but it was considered that some such facilities had probably developed in the areas covered between 1976 and 1981 (the date of publication).

The biggest providers of day services were social services departments (47 per cent), followed by health authorities (26 per cent), voluntary organisations (23 per cent) and finally, other statutory agencies (4 per cent). The range of types of day centres made it difficult for general comments to be made on management, but the study was extensively reported and there was detailed discussion of each type of unit. Some of the comments on possible improvements (for example the suggestion that there was some scope for users to manage units themselves) could have relevance to the level of violence, but violence itself was hardly mentioned in the report. Physical fights did occur in some ATCs, but almost never between users and staff (Carter, 1981, p. 306). Because the issue was hardly raised it is not surprising that there was no discussion of the prevention and management of violence. However, in considering regimes and the aims of day centres and day hospitals, the study makes an excellent starting point. In a chapter entitled 'Room for Improvement', Carter presented comments that she had received from users and staff about the changes they would like to have seen in their day units. The comments were grouped according to the following topics: the programme (work, social activities, treatment, arts and crafts, meetings and groups, education), the users and the regime (including comments on greater participation in management), the building, the facilities, the staff, the organisation. A more detailed analysis of the data from the project can be found in an associated publication (Edwards and Carter, 1980). This provides a framework on which users, staff and management could base their discussions when creating, analysing or changing various aspects of a day centre.

Where staff wish to create a particular type of regime, specialist groups or publications may be of interest. Therapeutic community ideas have an influence in some day care settings, and Blake and Millard (1979) edited a booklet which outlines some of the basic principles that have especially influenced mental health day centres in Britain. When different kinds of regime are being considered in the process of deciding on aims and priorities, their various implications for the prevention and management of violence should always be taken into account.

General considerations

We have previously noted the importance of recording and reporting in the management of potential violence. The files of people thought likely to behave aggressively should be marked accordingly, and reviewed regularly by the responsible staff member and the line manager. If incidents of violence do occur, it is particularly important that they are reported, and if people or property have been harmed, a record should be made in the accident book. In residential and day care centres, such records provide essential information for staff who come on duty after an incident. In all social work settings, records provide managers with an indication of the extent of the problem, and the reluctance of staff to report incidents appears to have led to a serious underestimate of the amount of violence that is experienced in agencies. Furthermore, under-reporting in-hibits the process of learning from events, and a wealth of practical knowledge is lost thereby.

The identification of situations in which staff may be placed at risk leads us to consider the process by which managers allocate work to staff in the first place. Many team leaders will have seen the publicity given in December 1983 to a case where a social worker had been raped by a client, and received an out of court settlement from her local authority of £30 000. Fogerty noted that the social worker claimed that as she was not qualified, she should not have been asked to visit the man, given what was known of his history: 'Had the case been brought to the court, the costs to the local authority could have been a good deal higher if negligence were proven. If an unqualified social worker is sent out to interview a client with a history of mental illness and is attacked, is there a case for sueing the employer on grounds of negligence?' She continued:

> A qualification in social work will, of course, be of limited use when pitted against a fifteen stone man who lashes out. But if a worker is 'qualified' to carry out the practice of social work, with all its associated risks, the grounds for sueing an employer for negligence are considerably diminished. If a client has a history of extreme violence and the social worker is still sent out alone to interview him, then the case against the employer for negligence is fairly (although not absolutely) clear. The social worker should have had an escort and by failing to provide that facility the local authority could be seen to be negligent. (Fogerty, 1983, p. 6)

Where there is a known risk of violence, therefore, the manager must think about who to send on a visit, where the interview should take place and whether or not to send an escort. If staff are interviewing in the office out of normal hours, are they ever left alone, or is there always some back up? The position of students on placement seems to vary considerably between agencies, but staff should know if there is a clear policy on the type of work that can be allocated to students, and whether they are covered by insurance arrangements within the agency.

This brings us to a central dilemma for social workers faced with violent situations and deciding whether to ask for help. At one level, social workers could often be seen as ill-suited to dealing with violent situations. Jordan and Packman (1978) and then Prins (1980) considered that the personalities of many social workers might not be fitted to taking part in violent confrontation. They often lack the confidence and size of police constables. 'In fact, the opposite may be nearer the truth, for by and large social workers are likely to be recruited from the ranks of the introverted and possibly less physically robust.' However, in the next sentence Prins introduced the dilemma: 'It may be that social workers and others are sometimes particularly effective in these explosive situations, because, unlike officers of the law, they are in no position to enforce or carry through any kind of physical submission. They have only themselves and their personal skills to rely upon. They may, therefore, be the best people to open up lines of communication.' (Prins, 1980, p. 187)

Prins then examined some of the attributes he considered essential for those working with dangerous clients or in potentially violent situations. These included abilities in respect of the following: honesty and acknowledging one's own potential for violence; avoiding panic, taking a rounded and objective view of the dangerous person; intervening directly where appropriate; being responsive to pleas for help and looking out for warning signs. Drawing on his earlier work with Packman, Jordan concluded that 'the physically weak but morally courageous are often most successful in dealing with alarmingly violent situations'. (Jordan, 1984, p. 160)

The stereotyping of police and social workers should be avoided; instead, it is important to look at skills and methods employed. The recent BBC series on the police showed an incident where apparently rather heavy-handed methods were used to deal with a man reported to be blockaded in his house with a shot-gun. Jordan's example might appear to indicate an alternative, social work approach:

> A young woman, who was then an unqualified social work trainee, was called to the scene of a siege, by policemen and Alsatian dogs, of a house where a man with a shotgun was barricaded with his wife and children. The man had originally threatened an official of the Electricity Board who had come to disconnect their supply. The social worker asked the police to withdraw (which they did under protest) gained access to the house simply by walking up to the door, and found that the man was (after initial suspicion) very willing to talk to her. She was able eventually to negotiate a settlement with the Electricity Board. (Jordan, 1984, pp. 160–1)

However, it is essential to recognise both the risks involved and the fact that many police are especially skilled in the 'softly, softly' approach, while some social workers may be prone to overreaction and a heavier response. Many of those interviewed in the Wessex study stated that they generally found the police to be good at defusing situations and calmly but firmly restoring order. The personality, approach, skill and judgement of the individual is the common element.

Mental disorder

There is a considerable volume of literature on social work and mental disorder, and much of it includes an examination of the process of compulsory admission to psychiatric hospital. However, the issue of violence towards the social worker and how to deal with it is rarely covered. This is perhaps a little surprising, given the size of the problem indicated by the Wessex study. It is hoped that the guidelines together with the suggestions for training given elsewhere in this book will help to redress this balance.

Prins has at least considered the more general issue of the social worker's role in dealing with the potentially violent patient. He identified the need to take detailed social histories and to look for warning signs. He looked at the interview process itself and the need sometimes to ask more direct questions (Prins, 1975, p. 305). His guidance on predicting violence towards others and his proposals for preventive action have been challenged by Webb as relying too heavily on post hoc explanations (Webb, 1976, p. 91). Not related directly to assaults on social workers is a range of literature on the prediction of dangerousness, and managing violence (Greenland, 1978; Megargee, 1979; Rappaport, 1967).

Private and voluntary homes

The private and voluntary sectors were grossly under-represented in the Wessex study but have, of course, increased quite dramatically over the last few years. Much of the comment above will be of relevance, but it is worth noting that there is specific reference to the problem of violence in private and voluntary homes in the guidelines produced by the Centre for Policy on Ageing. The guide, 'Home Life: a code of practice for residential care', is part of the government's plans to regulate residential care homes and to protect residents. It provides guidance for managers and home owners and for social services department staff who have to register and inspect the homes.

It is not surprising that the specific guidance is to be found in the section of the code that deals with elderly people with mental illness, as it is in this area that the number of such homes has increased very substantially, with a consequent increase in references to the problems of violence. The guidance itself is brief, but bears some relation to the examples of guidelines looked at earlier in Chapter 5. It starts from the position of maintaining control, a common theme, rather than in responding to violence that has been offered:

> When direction or control is necessary, it should be by means of tactful and sympathetic supervision and distraction. Physical restraint may constitute an assault and should be avoided except in the most urgent circumstances and in the interests of immediate safety. Any restraint should be temporary and medical advice must be sought at once. Restraint by sedation can only be applied by a medical practitioner. (Avebury, 1984, p. 46)

Elsewhere in the guide, there is an expectation that social services departments may well have their own clearly worked out and documented ideas on dealing with violence. In producing a list of what should be sent to inquiring prospective proprietors of rest homes, the guide refers to various legal documents and then to: 'Notes of guidance on specific matters which may have been formulated locally' including 'a policy statement about the methods of controlling disruptive residents in children's homes or homes for mentally handicapped people' (Avebury, 1984, p. 56). It is almost certainly over-optimistic to assume that such notes of guidance exist in most authorities. We hope that the right balance will be struck, in the majority of cases, between reducing the risk to staff and protecting the rights of residents. We hope that the training encouraged by the code will address these issues but it is hard to imagine such training being funded from registration fees, given the level at which they have been set. There is a real danger that some of the worst experiences of residents and staff in hospitals may be translated into the new front line of community care, unless the conditions under which rest homes operate are carefully monitored.

Conclusions

This chapter has sought to highlight issues that should concern managers in a range of different social work settings. This has been a somewhat arbitrary process, because the entire book is in one sense addressed to managers as well as to practitioners. In conclusion, therefore, we have extrapolated a 'Checklist for Managers' to use in reviewing what their agency is doing to minimise risks to staff:

Staffing
- Does the establishment have sufficient staff?
- Is care taken to appoint appropriate staff?
- Are staff given training in the reduction of violence?
- Do all staff feel supported, secure and able to admit fears and report violent incidents?
- Does the agency provide clear practice guidelines for staff?
- Are the provisions of the Health and Safety at Work legislation being complied with?
- Are staff properly insured against the risk of assault?

The working environment
- Are reception areas, interviewing rooms and other facilities designed and furnished so as to provide security for all who use them?
- Are there alarm systems, and do staff know how to use them?
- Is there a system of 'coded' messages requesting assistance?
- Is care taken to exclude objects that are potential weapons?

The agency's
task

- Are all staff kept aware of the dangers of known 'high-risk' procedures? (compulsory admissions to care, hospitals, homes).
- Are agency records used systematically to identify those who may become violent?
- Is it the practice that staff are never left alone in a building?
- In fieldwork settings, is care taken:
    To allocate work appropriately?
    To decide whether 'paired' home visits or office interviews are necessary?
    To decide whether police assistance is required?
    To decide whether standby staff and pre-arranged interruptions should be organised in office interviews?
- In residential and day care settings, is care taken:
    To develop and maintain an ethos that will minimise risk?
    To facilitate communication between staff and residents?
    To work out rotas and staff combinations that will reduce risks of confrontation?
- After incidents of violence,
    Are staff given proper support?
    Are incidents recorded and reported?
    Is the question of prosecuting the assailant considered?

8

Training Implications

It is no exaggeration to state that training is the basis of both
prevention and management. This chapter is therefore concerned with training social work staff to anticipate and deal
competently with the threat of violence. We shall firstly
consider the need for training, and then move on to look at
some relevant principles, the content of training programmes,
and methods of training, including some that we have tried.

The need for training

It is rarely difficult to argue a convincing case for more
training, especially in a subject as sensitive as violence towards
staff. So it is as well to remind ourselves that 82 per cent of
respondents in the Wessex study reported that their training
had given them no guidance in the practical management of
violence. Comparing different groups, we found that less than
one in seven fieldworkers had had such training; the position
was only slightly better for day care staff (one in five) and
residential workers (one in four). We cannot prove that
training helps staff to cope more effectively with dangerous
situations, but it is surely self-evident that the staff of social
work agencies should be absolutely clear about what they are
expected to do when threatened with violence. This point is
certainly becoming recognised in the health sector; in our
earlier discussion of guidelines, in Chapter 5, John Martin's
recent study of hospital enquiries was quoted: 'it is important
to consider the implications of violent incidents in terms of . . .

providing some training for all grades' (1984, p. 239, our italics).

The importance of learning to handle aggression was demonstrated recently when the administrative, secretarial and clerical staff of a county probation service (Oxfordshire) were able to choose the subject for their first in-service training day; they opted overwhelmingly for 'Dealing with difficult and aggressive clients'. This choice reflected not only their feelings about potential violence, but also the fact that they encounter aggression with some frequency, at the reception desk and when answering the telephone. Their concern is reflected in a new document on probation training needs produced by chief probation officers:

> It is clear that at least some clerical staff, such as receptionists, require at least a minimum provision of training for handling clients sometimes in difficult situations. Commonsense – not to mention health and safety regulations – demands that staff who have any prospect of finding themselves in that situation should be prepared for it. (ACOP, 1984, p. 7)

This statement reminds us that such training is not merely desirable, it is a legal obligation under the 1974 Health and Safety at Work Act. The Act places a duty on the employer to provide 'such . . . training . . . as is necessary to ensure . . . the safety at work of his employees' (Section 2(2) (C)).

Training is therefore required by law for employees whose safety may be threatened. John Martin's comment, referring to the hospital context, suggested that such training should be provided 'for all grades'. In the context of social work, we suggest that training is needed for a very wide range of staff, including the clerical staff mentioned above and the residential, day care, fieldwork and management staff discussed in earlier chapters. Some of these groups will have undertaken pre-professional training courses such as CQSW and CSS, and so it is essential that such courses include material on handling aggression, a subject about which many students are concerned. But pre-professional training cannot meet the needs of all staff, and the obvious implication of the 1974 Act's stress on the employer is that this kind of training must be provided on an 'in-service' basis.

A final comment about training needs is that the specific risks faced by particular groups should always be acknowledged. One of the most important points to emerge from Chapter 1 was the identification of the dangers associated with taking children into care, and with the compulsory hospital admission of mentally disordered persons. The chapter also pointed out that fieldworkers may be assaulted in the office, during a home visit or in a car or ambulance, and in some of these situations they may find themselves alone. Likewise, social work staff based in general and psychiatric hospitals face risks specific to those settings. Similar comments can be made about most groups of staff, but in the Wessex study it was noteworthy that fieldworkers received even less training in dealing with violence than did residential and day care staff.

Some relevant principles

In this section we suggest that the following nine principles should underpin training programmes concerned with handling aggression:

(i) People's anxieties and fears should be recognised and used;

(ii) People's own aggressive feelings should be acknowledged;

(iii) Training should be based on identified needs;

(iv) Training should enable people to learn from experience;

(v) Training should focus on prevention;

(vi) The entire staff of an office/centre/home should be involved;

(vii) The question of who should lead the programme needs careful consideration;

(viii) Clarity of presentation is essential;

(ix) Training should seek to develop both knowledge and skills.

While many of these principles apply generally in social work training, we include the list at this point simply because we have found them indispensable in organising our own training programmes concerned with aggression; the reader may well be able to add more. The first principle involves recognising the anxiety that is associated with violence, and using this anxiety creatively in training sessions. For anyone who is organising training, the attraction of a session on violence is the ease with which the attention of an audience can be gained. It is hard to think of many other subjects in which real anxieties can be so quickly aroused. For this reason any exploration of violence needs to be planned with great care, so that course members are not left feeling disturbed and uncertain.

Linked with this comment is the second principle, that the aggressive feelings of course members themselves should be acknowledged. This point was made strongly to us by a group of receptionists, as they described their anger towards social workers who left them alone to cope with difficult and aggressive people. We have also noted earlier in this book that violence may be reciprocal in some day centres and residential settings, and our focus on violence towards staff must not obscure the fact that nobody is immune from aggressive impulses.

We noted in Chapter 4 that training should be planned in response to identified needs, and that line managers have a role in identifying those needs. If an incident of threatened or actual violence occurs in a centre or office, its lessons should be incorporated into in-service training. We suggested in Chapter 6 that discussion after the event, in addition to meeting the needs of the victim, could usefully focus on the way in which the incident developed and was handled; obviously such discussion requires care and sensitivity, but when properly managed it can be invaluable in suggesting ideas for training. A recent illustration of this process in our own experience was provided by a principal area officer who described to a group of social work students an incident in her office. She mentioned that she had learned always to call the police on '999' rather than the ordinary station number. In some police areas '999' calls are tape-recorded, and if it is necessary to speak softly, the message can easily be replayed at a higher volume. This example incidentally demonstrates the value of involving people with practical experience in training, and reinforces our earlier comments about the value of maintaining good relationships with the police.

We have reached the fourth principle, that training should seek to discover, share and utilise the collective experience and practice wisdom of course members. A theme of this book is that social work staff generally handle threatening incidents very well, but the skills used in handling aggression are rarely discussed and shared.

The fifth principle, that training should emphasise prevention, does not require much comment, since the object of training must be to maximise the extent of good practice in working with people who may be disturbed and aggressive. Because violence can be sensational and even entertaining, it is important to bear in mind the mundane but vital theme of prevention when planning training programmes. The sixth principle, that the entire staff of a work centre should be involved in in-service training events, is perhaps rather less obvious. One of the greatest obstacles to the spreading of good practice is poor communication within social work agencies, particularly between different levels of a hierarchy. Staff who encounter aggression may not report it for fear of appearing incompetent; management, in the absence of evidence to the contrary, will assume that violence is not a problem in their agency. In our training experience, junior clerical staff have used anonymous posters and drawings to communicate fear, anxiety and anger to their managers, who have in turn been able to respond constructively. Staff need to know that they will be supported and not criticised when they report incidents and threats; female staff must be certain that their reports of obscene telephone calls will be accepted seriously, and with sensitivity rather than light amusement.

A staff group often forgotten in training programmes devised for social work and management staff are receptionists and telephonists. They should be included, not only for the reasons just mentioned, but also because they have much to contribute. It is instructive to ask an experienced receptionist to describe in detail how she (or he, but the majority are female) has dealt with those who are particularly disturbed or aggressive. Such descriptions will commonly include simple practicalities like talking quietly, listening attentively, behaving calmly, smiling and perhaps offering to make a hot drink. Such behaviour is justified by social psychology as well as common sense.

Linked with the question of who should take part in training events is that of who should lead them. If training is organised within a particular agency, it may make it easier for staff to share feelings, including criticisms of colleagues and seniors, if the session is led by someone neutral from outside the agency. It can be inhibiting, to say the least, if a team senior or principal officer takes charge.

The eighth principle concerns clarity. For good reasons, simple, firm guidelines about what to do in particular situations are not common in social work textbooks. When violence is threatened, however, staff do need to know what is appropriate and permissible; 86 per cent of respondents in the Wessex study took the view that printed guidelines on the management of violence should be made available. Training organisers may consider that simple models of aggressive behaviour, such as the 'Arousal – trigger – weapon – target' model outlined in Chapter 2, are easily learned and are probably more relevant in situations of stress than the more academic concepts of Freud and others. The training of people to cope with rare but potentially life-threatening events should seek to impart clear and memorable concepts, and perhaps social work staff can learn from those who teach techniques of first aid and artificial respiration.

The final principle we suggest is that training should enable people to develop both their knowledge and their skills. This brings us to consider the content of training.

The content of training programmes

The plan of this book has been developed from a set of guidelines written in response to the needs of staff. Our answer to the question 'What do staff need to know about violent incidents?' would therefore be suggested by the book's contents. Chapters 2 to 5 represent an implicit four-stage model that could be used in designing a training event:

    (i)   Understanding the causes of violence;
   (ii) Recognising potential violence;
  (iii) Preventing violence;
  (iv) What to do if violence occurs.

The sixth chapter, 'What support should I expect?', contains material for several sessions; coping with fear and guilt, the role of managers, trade unions and professional organisations, statistics, external help, legal and financial help. Likewise, the subheadings of other chapters suggest further possibilities, from reception arrangements to the practicalities and legal aspects of physical restraint. Chapters 1 and 7 contain material relevant to particular settings. The choice of subjects for a particular programme should, as we have noted, be determined by the identified needs of those participating. Chapter 1 includes a list of the concerns of those who teach the mentally handicapped, and from that list it is possible to identify their particular needs for knowledge, which include procedures in difficult situations, the law relating to coping with violence, and the law relating to compensation for both physical injury and damage to property. In addition there was a need for specific information about alarm systems, and about trainees. It should not be too difficult to incorporate this kind of knowledge and information into training programmes.

It is perhaps less easy to identify the skills demanded by situations of potential violence. De Felippo's list of ground rules for psychiatric nurses (Chapter 4) gives some clues; the skills involved might include maintaining appropriate physical distance from the patient, awareness of their behavioural clues, the ability to demonstrate control supported by sanctions if necessary, skill in using physical activity to direct aggression, the ability to use humour in defusing tension, and the ability to feel secure with impulsive patients. These skills may seem rather diffuse, but they are in fact concerned with the vital details of staff behaviour. A similar list for residential staff was mentioned in Chapter 5:

(i)   Anticipation;
(ii) Acting decisively and effectively;
(iii) Providing 'time out';
(iv) Physical containment;
(v)   Explicit approach.

(Payne and Douglas, 1981)

This list suggests itself as a framework for a training session, and would need to be followed by a programme which aimed to develop these skills.

In this section we have asserted that training events should seek both to impart knowledge and to develop skills. These twin objectives have become common in social work training, and in the next section we shall consider how they may be achieved.

Methods of training

Once the knowledge and skills content of a training programme have been determined on the basis of identified needs, it is appropriate to consider training resources. These are likely to include books, other printed material such as guidelines, audio-visual material such as video films, and people with relevant experience to share. Ideas for books and articles may be suggested by the list of references at the end of this book. The Wessex study revealed a strong desire for clear guidelines, and training organisers might wish to consider providing such material for participants in advance of a training event, or alternatively giving handouts for people to keep for future reference. The DHSS and COHSE guidelines discussed in Chapter 5 provide one model, and another is represented by the Hampshire guidelines quoted later in the same chapter. These were written by Stanley Bute in 1980 for Hampshire County Council, and have aroused widespread interest in other authorities.

Video material designed to supplement training programmes on violence is now becoming available, and at the time of writing we are aware of three films on the market. The authors' 'Violence – its prevention and management' was produced at the beginning of 1983 in response to an apparent need for such material, and demand for it has been heavy despite limited advertising. The first part of the film depicts a fictional violent incident in an social services office, and is designed to stimulate discussion in a audience. The second part of the film, intended for use later in the session, draws some very simple lessons from the violent incident. Since its production, the East Sussex Consultancy and Training Agency has produced a much more substantial video-assisted training package, 'Handling Aggression and Conflict', which contains sufficient material for a five-day course. The package deals with aggression by adolescents in residential establishments, and the video film depicts a violent incident in a children's home with five 'cameos' of incidents that are common in residential work. The third and most recent film, 'Understanding and handling aggression', is presented by Malcolm Brown, lasts for fifty-two minutes and is available from Tavistock Publications. Further such material may be in the course of preparation.

These films contain examples of bad practice leading to violence, and apart from the obvious message they convey, it is worth noticing that many audiences appear to learn more easily from bad practice than from examples of situations handled well; it is generally easier to criticise (and dissociate oneself from the consequences) than it is to identify why a particular intervention proved effective. It should also be remembered that video films, like other training materials, inevitably reflect the attitudes and values of those who produced them, attitudes and values which a training organiser may not share.

Books, articles, films and people with experience of handling violence can all be used to provide the kind of knowledge and information discussed in the last section. They can also be used to stimulate interest and discussion in an audience, but they are less useful for the purpose of encouraging skill development. Role-play is often suggested as a good way of achieving this objective, but we have found that it needs to be used with great care, for two reasons. Firstly, and obviously, it can easily get out of hand and become too realistic, so that people are hurt emotionally and perhaps physically. Secondly, role-play can demonstrate that it is much more difficult to deal with aggression than one might think, and this discovery can be extremely dispiriting. With these provisos, role-play can usefully be employed in conjunction with other learning methods.

Other learning methods include the increasingly popular 'social skills' approach. One of the few books familiar in social work that has relevance to difficulties of handling aggression is *Social Skills and Personal Problem Solving* (Priestley *et al.*, 1978). Dealing with violence, in oneself and others, is suggested as one of a number of subjects which can usefully be tackled from a social skills perspective. It is interesting to note that the book mentions a learning theorist, Bandura, as one of its source suggestions. The book does not go into detail on the subject of violence, but it does offer a framework around which a training programme may be devised:

    (i)   Identify the aims of the programme;
   (ii)   Provide a stimulus to learning;
  (iii) Introduce assessment methods, designed to enable people to explore their own responses;
  (iv) Encourage people to set themselves learning objectives;
   (v) Introduce a range of relevant learning procedures;
  (vi) Evaluate what has been learned.

The aims of a violence programme might be to find and practice methods of controlling violence, to help people explore their own aggressive feelings, and to understand the effects of violence on themselves and others. Stimulus material could include a film, a cartoon, a description of a violent event, or a role-play. The book suggests a very wide range of practical methods which can help people to identify their problems, weaknesses and strengths, as a vital prelude to the actual learning process. There is an equally wide range of suggestions for learning factual information, confronting attitudes and developing skills. Finally there are some ideas for evaluating the effectiveness of the programme.

One of the advantages of the social skills approach is that it can be used by anyone, staff, clients, residents and so on. In the long run, it is clearly desirable to teach people how to handle their own aggressive feelings, rather than to teach potential victims how to protect themselves; social skills and similar forms of training have much to contribute in residential work with children and young people.

In the Wessex study, residential and day care staff showed a significant interest in the techniques of physical restraint. The guidelines cited in Chapter 5 described some of these techniques, and elsewhere in the chapter the legal aspects of restraint are discussed. It may well be that a training programme on violence needs to include teaching the skills of restraint, and it is not easy to suggest sources of expertise in an area where many training departments and institutions have no experience. If there are no suitably qualified staff in the agency concerned, it may be necessary to go further afield, for example to a psychiatric hospital, to find people who can give appropriate advice.

We now turn to our own experience of training staff to anticipate and respond appropriately to the threat of violence. The following model for a half-day session includes elements of the social skills approach. We have used it, with variations, on a number of occasions involving the in-service training of mixed staff groups. It is one of numerous possibilities, and may stimulate ideas for different programmes:

I   Short introduction, setting out the aim of the session; to enable people to learn from the collective experience of the group.

II   Stimulus material; video film depicting a violent incident.

III Exercises in groups: i) Identify factors causing the violence;

                        ii) Group members depict personal experiences and feelings of aggression on large sheets of paper.

IV 'Market-place'; informal prelude to plenary session in which people view and discuss all the depictions.

V   Plenary session, identifying themes and general issues about the handling of aggression by reference to the depictions.

VI Second part of video film, which reinforces and adds to the plenary discussion as it makes general points by reference back to the original incident.

When using this model with a group of CQSW students, who may not have any relevant experience, we have found it helpful to invite someone who has experienced violence to come and describe it for a few minutes. The model is planned around our own film, the second half of which was designed to emphasise and confirm the various points which the first half usually elicits.

When planning such programmes, it is important to recognise that they can be the first occasion when individuals talk about painful incidents in which they have been involved. They can also provide the first opportunity for people to speak openly to senior staff about weaknesses in the organisation. This may take the form of something simple but important – 'no-one told the new staff that we have an alarm system' – or more emotive – 'my chief officer told me that it was my fault that I had been attacked'. Both these remarks were made in recent training sessions.

Conclusions

This chapter has adopted a four part approach to the question of training. It began by stressing the significance of training, a subject mentioned in each of the preceding four chapters and a legal requirement with regard to safety at work. Nine principles for training were then proposed, and the content of training in terms of knowledge and skills was discussed. Finally some materials and methods were suggested. In conclusion, we reiterate the importance of sensitivity in planning training sessions. Sensitivity is essential if the unnecessary creation of defensiveness is to be avoided, the feeling that 'we' must protect ourselves from 'them'. To build such barriers can be to destroy the social work profession's best defence against violence, the quality of relationships between staff and those they seek to help. It is dangerously easy to arouse anxiety in ways that help neither staff nor clients. To hear accounts or witness films of violent incidents can be very frightening for staff who may be facing disturbed, distraught or drunken people at work next day. Any detailed consideration of violent events must be placed firmly in the context of the fact that every day, thousands of potential outbursts are defused calmly and competently by staff across the whole range of day care, residential and fieldwork services. The objective of training must always be to extend that competence towards the relatively small number of occasions when things go wrong. This book has been written as a contribution towards that objective.

Appendix: The Criminal Injuries Compensation Scheme

The extracts given here* summarise the main features of the scheme. Prospective applicants should obtain full information from the Criminal Injuries Compensation Board.

* * *

Requests for application forms and all inquiries should be addressed to:

Criminal Injuries Compensation Board,
10-12 Russell Square,
LONDON WC1B 5EN
Tel. 01-636 2812
01-636 4201

Scope of the Scheme

4. The Board will entertain applications for *ex gratia* payments of compensation in any case where the applicant or, in the case of application by a spouse or dependant (see paragraph 15 . . . below), the deceased, sustained in Great Britain . . . personal injury directly attributable

    (a) to a crime of violence (including arson or poisoning) or

*Source: Cmnd 9093, HMSO, 1983.

(b) to the apprehension or attempted apprehension of an offender or a suspected offender or to the prevention or attempted prevention of an offence or to the giving of help to any constable who is engaged in any such activity.

Applications for compensation will be entertained only if made within three years of the incident giving rise to the injury, except that the Board may in exceptional cases waive this requirement. A decision by the Chairman not to waive the time limit will be final. In considering for the purpose of this paragraph whether any act is a criminal act, any immunity at law of an offender, attributable to his youth or insanity or other conclusion, will be left out of account.

5. Compensation will not be payable unless the Board are satisfied that the injury was one for which the total amount of compensation payable after deduction of social security benefits, but before any other deductions under the Scheme, would not be less than the minimum amount of compensation. This shall be £400 . . . The application of the minimum level shall not, however, affect the payment of funeral expenses under paragraph 15 below.

6. The Board may withhold or reduce compensation if they consider that –

(a) the applicant has not taken, without delay, all reasonable steps to inform the police, or any other authority considered by the Board to be appropriate for the purpose, of the circumstances of the injury and to co-operate with the police or other authority in bringing the offender to justice; or

(b) the applicant has failed to give all reasonable assistance to the Board or other authority in connection with the application; or

(c) having regard to the conduct of the applicant before, during or after the events giving rise to the claim to his character and way of life – and, in applications under paragraph 15 . . . below, to the character, conduct and way of life of the deceased and of the applicant – it is inappropriate that a full award, or any award at all, be granted.

Furthermore, compensation will not be payable –

(d) in the case of an application under paragraph 4 (b) above where the injury was sustained accidentally, unless the Board are satisfied that the applicant was at the time taking an exceptional risk which was justified in all the circumstances.

9. If in the opinion of the Board it is in the interests of the applicant (whether or not a minor or a person under an incapacity) so to do, the Board may pay the amount of any award to any trustee or trustees to hold on such trusts for the benefit of all or any of the following persons, namely the applicant and any spouse, widow or widower, relatives and dependants of the applicant and with such provisions for their respective maintenance, education and benefit and with such powers and provisions for the investment and management of the fund and for the remuneration of the trustee or trustees as the Board shall think fit. Subject to this the Board will have a general discretion in any case in which they have awarded compensation to make special arrangements for its administration.

10. The Board will consider applications for compensation arising out of acts of rape and other sexual offences both in respect of pain, suffering and shock and in respect of loss of earnings due to consequent pregnancy, and, where the victim is ineligible for a maternity grant under the National Insurance Scheme, in respect of the expenses of childbirth. Compensation will not be payable for the maintenance of any child born as a result of a sexual offence.

11. Applications for compensation for personal injury attributable to traffic offences will be excluded from the Scheme, except where such injury is due to a deliberate attempt to run the victim down.

Basis of compensation

12. Subject to the other provisions of this Scheme, compensation will be assessed on the basis of common law damages and will normally take the form of a lump sum payment, although the Board may make alternative arrangements in accordance with paragraph 9 above. More than one payment may be made where an applicant's eligibility for compensation has been established but a final award cannot be calculated in the first instance – for example, where only a provisional medical assessment can be given. In a case in which an interim award has been made, the Board may decide to make a reduced award, increase any reduction already made or refuse to make any further payment at any stage before receiving notification of acceptance of a final award.

13. Although the Board's decisions in a case will normally be final, they will have discretion to reconsider a case after a final award of compensation has been accepted where there has been such a serious change in the applicant's medical condition that injustice would occur if the original assessment of compensation were allowed to stand, or where the victim has since died as a result of his injuries. A case will not be re-opened more than three years after the date of the final award unless the Board are satisfied, on the basis of evidence presented with the application for re-opening the case, that the renewed application can be considered without a need for extensive enquiries. A decision by the Chairman that a case may not be re-opened will be final.

14. Compensation will be limited as follows:–

(a) the rate of net loss of earnings or earning capacity to be taken into account shall not exceed twice the gross average industrial earnings at the date of assessment (as published in the Department of Employment Gazette and adjusted as considered appropriate by the Board);

(b) there shall be no element comparable to exemplary or punitive damages.

15. Where the victim has died in consequence of the injury, no compensation other than funeral expenses will be payable for the benefit of his estate, but the Board will be able to entertain applications from any person who is a dependant of the victim . . . Compensation will be payable in accordance with the other provisions of this Scheme to any such dependant or relative. Funeral expenses to an amount considered reasonable by the Board will be paid in appropriate cases, even where the person bearing the cost of the funeral is otherwise ineligible to claim under this Scheme. Applications may be made under this paragraph where the victim has died from his injuries even if an award has been made to the victim in his lifetime. Such cases will be subject to the conditions set out in paragraph 13 for the re-opening of cases and compensation payable to the applicant will be reduced by the amount paid to the victim.

17. Compensation will be payable for loss of or damage to clothing and other personal adjuncts arising from the injury. Personal adjuncts do not include jewellery, watches or rings lost or damaged, whether at the time of the offence or afterwards or in the course of medical or other treatment arising from the offence. Save as aforesaid, compensation will not be payable for loss of or damage to property.

18. The cost of private medical treatment will be payable by the Board only if the Board consider that, in all the circumstances, both the private treatment and the cost of it are reasonable.

19. Compensation will be reduced by the full value of any present or future entitlement to:–

(a) UK social security benefits

(b) compensation awards under the Criminal Injuries (Compensation) (Northern Ireland) Order 1977

(c) social security benefits, compensation awards or similar payments whatsoever from the funds of other countries, or

(d) payments under insurance arrangements except as excluded below which may accrue, as a result of the injury or death, to the benefit of the person to whom the award is made.

Procedure for determining applications

22. Every application will be made to the Board in writing as soon as possible after the event on a form obtainable from the Board's office. The initial decision on the amount of any compensation awarded will be taken by one member of the Board and where an award is made the applicant will be given a breakdown of the assessment of compensation, except where the Board consider this inappropriate, where an award is refused or reduced, reasons for the decision will be given. If the applicant is not satisfied with the decision, he will be entitled to a hearing before three members of the Board other than the member who made the initial decision. An application for a hearing must be made within three months of notification of the initial decision.

NOTE: Injured persons can obtain details of DHSS industrial injury benefits from leaflet FB.2 (revised November 1985) and leaflets NI. 6, NI. 10, NI. 16 and NI. 244.

References

Association of Chief Officers of Probation (1984) *Probation Service Training Needs Now*, ACOP, 6 February 1984.

Altschuler, K. Z. (1962) Article in *American Annals of the Deaf* 107, 1962.

Ardrey, R. (1961) *African Genesis*, New York, Atheneum.

Ardrey, R. (1966) *The Territorial Imperative*, London, Collins.

Avebury, Kina, Lady (1984) *Home Life: a Code of Practice for Residential Care*, London, Centre for Policy on Ageing.

Bailey, R. H. (1977) *Violence and Aggression*, Time-Life (Nederland) B.V.

Bandura, A. (1973a) *Aggression: A Social Learning Analysis*, New Jersey, Prentice-Hall.

Bandura, A. (1973b) *Social Learning Analysis of Aggression*, Paper presented at the Meeting of the American Psychological Association, Montreal, September 1973.

Barclay, P. (1982) *Social Workers: Their Role and Tasks*, London, National Institute for Social Work, Bedford Square Press.

Belson, W. A. (1978) *Television Violence and the Adolescent Boy*, Farnborough, Saxon House.

Berkowitz, L. (1973) 'Simple Views of Aggression' in Montagu, A. (ed.) *Man and Aggression*, 2nd edition, New York, Oxford University Press.

Bernstein, B. (1981) 'Survey of Threats and Assaults directed towards Psychotherapists', *American Journal of Psychotherapy* 34, October 1981.

Blake, R. and Millard, D. (ed.) (1979) *The Therapeutic Community in Day Care*, London, Association of Therapeutic Communities.

Boulding, K. E. (1973) 'Am I a Man or a Mouse – or Both?' in Montagu, A. (ed.) *Man and Aggression*, 2nd edition, New York, Oxford University Press.

Bowden, P. (1978) 'The Psychology of Violence', *Nursing Mirror* 146, 15 June 1978.

Brailsford, D. S. and Stevenson, J. (1973) 'Factors related to Violent and Unpredictable Behaviour in Psychiatric Hospitals', *Nursing Times*, 69 (3) 1973.

Brearley, C. P. *et al.* (1980) *Admission to Residential Care*, London, Tavistock.

Brown, J. A. C. (1961) *Freud and the Post-Freudians*, Harmondsworth, Penguin.

Bute, S. F. (1979a) Unpublished paper, Bristol University Personal Social Services Fellowship, July 1979.

Bute, S. F. (1979b) 'The Threat of Violence in Close Encounters with Clients', *Social Work Today*, 11 (14), 4 December 1979.

Bute, S. F. (1980) *Staff Guidelines on the Management of Violence*, Hampshire Social Services, May 1980.

Cannon, W. B. (1924) *Bodily Changes in Pain, Hunger, Fear and Rage*, New York, Appleton.

Carson, D. (1983) 'Mental Processes: the Mental Health Act 1983', *The Journal of Social Welfare Law*, 1983, 195–211.

Carter, J. (1981) *Day Services for Adults*, London, National Institute for Social Work.

Clarke, R. and Sinclair, I. (1970) *Literature Survey on Aggression*, Home Office (unpublished).

Coffey, M. P. (1976) 'The Violent Patient', *Journal of Advanced Nursing*, 1976 (1), 341–50.

Comber, L. C. and Whitfield, R. C. (1979) *Action on Indiscipline*, National Association of Schoolmasters and Union of Women Teachers.

Confederation of Health Service Employees (1977) *The Management of Violent or Potentially Violent Patients*, Banstead, COHSE.

Criminal Injuries Compensation Board (1983) *19th Report*, HMSO Cmnd. 9093, November 1983.

Crine, A. (1982) 'An Occupational Hazard', *Community Care* 437, 11 November 1982.

Crook, J. H. (1973) 'The Nature and Function of Territorial Aggression' in Montagu, A. (ed.) *Man and Aggression*, 2nd edition, New York, Oxford University Press.

Denmark, J. C. (1966) 'Mental Illness and Early Profound Deafness', *British Journal of Medical Psychology*, 39, 1966, 121.

Denmark, J. C. and Eldridge, R. W. (1969) 'Psychiatric Services for the Deaf', *The Lancet*, 2 August 1969.

Denmark, J. C. (1972) 'Surdophrenia', *Sound*, 6, 1972, 97–8.

Department of Health and Social Security (1976) *The Management of Violent, or potentially Violent, Hospital Patients*, Health Circular (76) 11, March 1976.

Doyle, C. and Oates, M. R. (1980) 'Child Abuse – Focus on Good Practice', *Social Work Today*, 12 (5), 30 September 1980.

Edelman, S. (1978) 'Managing the Violent Patient in a Community Mental Health Centre', *Hospital and Community Psychiatry*, 29, July 1978.

Edwards, C. and Carter, J. (1980) *The Data of Day Care*, London, National Institue for Social Work.

De Felippo, A. M. (1976) 'Preventing Assaultive Behaviour on a Psychiatric Unit', *Supervisor Nurse*, 7 (6), June 1976.

Floud, J. and Young, W. (1983) *Dangerousness and Criminal Justice*, Cambridge Studies in Criminology, London, Heinemann.

Fogerty, M. (1983) 'Risks of Social Work', *Social Work Today*, 15 (16), 20 December 1983.

Fottrell, E. (1980) 'A Study of Violent Behaviour among Patients in Psychiatric Hospitals', *British Journal of Psychiatry*, 136, 1980.

Freud, S. (1918) Reflections on War and Death, New York, Moffat, Yard.

Freud, S. (1920) *Beyond the Pleasure Principle*, London, Institute of Psychoanalysis, Hogarth Press.

Freud, S. (1930) *Civilisation and its Discontents*, London, Hogarth Press.

Fry, A. (1983) 'Children who assaulted worker fined', *Community Care*, 485, 27 October 1983.

Green, S. (1982) 'Now I'm inclined to play it safe', *Community Care*, 437, 11 November 1982.

Greenland, C. (1978) 'The Prediction and Management of Violent Behaviour: Social Policy Issues', *International Journal of Law and Psychiatry*, 1978, 205–22.

Hall, A. S. (1974) *The Point of Entry*, London, George, Allen and Unwin.

Harrington, J. A. (1972) 'Hospital Violence', *Nursing Mirror*, 135, 3 and 4.

Harrison, P. (1974) 'The Old under Control', *New Society* 27 (591) 31 January 1974.

Hope, H. F. (1973) 'Trigger Factors', *Nursing Mirror*, 137, 20 July 1973.

Isaacs, S. (1972) 'Neglect, Cruelty and Battering', *British Medical Journal*, 3, 1972, 224–6.

Jordan, B. and Packman, J. (1978) 'Training for Social Work with Violent Families' in Martin, J. P. (ed.) *Violence and the Family*, Chichester, Wiley.

Jordan, B. (1984) *Invitation to Social Work*, Oxford, Martin Robertson.

Leavey, R. (1978) 'Violence in Community Homes', *Clearing House for Local Authority Social Services Research*, 8, 1978, 1–81, University of Birmingham.

Lefkowitz, M. M. *et al.* (1977) *Growing up to be Violent*, New York, Pergamon.

Liazos, A. (1977) 'The Poverty of the Sociology of Deviance: Nuts, Sluts and Perverts' in Fitzgerald, M. (ed.) *Welfare in Action*, London, Routledge and Kegan Paul.

Lorenz, K. (1966) *On Aggresssion*, London, Methuen.

Martin, J. P. (1984) *Hospitals in Trouble*, Oxford, Basil Blackwell.

Megargee, E. I. (1976) 'The Prediction of Violent Behaviour', *Criminal Justice and Behaviour*, 1976, 3–21.

Millham, S. *et al.* (1976) 'On Violence in Community Homes' in Tutt, N. (ed.) *Violence*, HMSO.

Millham, S., Bullock, R. and Hosie, K. (1978) *Locking up Children*, Farnborough, Saxon House.

Montagu, A. (ed.) (1973) *Man and Aggression*, 2nd edition, New York, Oxford University Press.

Montagu, A. (1978) *Learning Non-Aggression*, New York, Oxford University Press.

Morris, D. (1967) *The Naked Ape*, London, Jonathan Cape.

Morris, D. (1978) *Manwatching: A Field Guide to Human Behaviour*, London, Jonathan Cape.

Oates, M. R. (1979) 'Child Abuse and Neglect', *International Journal*, 3, 314, 1979, Pergamon.

Parker, T. and Allerton, R. (1962) *The Courage of his Convictions*, London, Hutchinson.

Payne, C. and Douglas, R. (1981) 'Planning to Deal with the Violent Ones', *Social Work Today*, 12 (38), 9 June 1981.

Penningroth, P. E. (1975) 'Control of Violence in a Mental Health Setting', *American Journal of Nursing*, 75 (4) April 1975.

Pithers, D. (1983) *Violence*, Unpublished paper given at Inter-disciplinary Conference on Violence in the Individual, Portman Clinic, 28 September 1983.

Powell, D. (1983) *Violence in Hostels for Adult Offenders*, Unpublished paper given at Inter-disciplinary Conference on Violence in the Individual, Portman Clinic, 28 September 1983.

Priestley, P. *et al.* (1978) *Social Skills and Personal Problem-Solving: A Handbook of Methods*, London, Tavistock.

Prins, H. (1975) 'A Danger to Themselves and Others', *British Journal of Social Work*, 1975, 297–309.

Prins, H. (1970) *Offenders, Deviants or Patients*, London, Tavistock.

Pulse Magazine (1984) 'Violence on Doctors', anonymous article, 9 June 1984.

Rappaport, J. R. (1967) *The Clinical Evaluation of the Dangerousness of the Mentally Ill*, Illinois, Charles C. Thomas.

Reid, J. A. (1973) 'Controlling the Fight/Flight Patient', *Canadian Nurse*, 69 (10), October 1973.

Report of the Committee of Inquiry into the Circumstances leading to the Death of Mr Daniel Carey at Tooting Bec Hospital on 2nd August 1974 (1975), London, South-West Thames Regional Health Authority.

Sears, R. R., Maccoby, E. E. and Levin, H. (1957) *Patterns of Child-Rearing*, New York, Row Peterson.

Star, B. (1983) 'Patient Violence/Therapist Safety', *Social Work*, 29 (3), May–June 1983, New York.

Stegne, L. R. (1978) 'A Positive Approach to Negative Behaviour', *Canadian Nurse*, 74 (6), June 1978.

Storr, A. (1968) *Human Aggression*, Harmondsworth, Penguin.

Taylor, P. (1983) 'Psychiatric Disorder and Crime' in Gibbons, J. L., *Psychiatry*, London, Heinemann.

Taylor, P. J. and Gunn, J. (1984) 'Violence and Psychosis', *British Medical Journal*, 288, 30 June 1984.

Walton, R. and Elliott, D. (eds) (1980) *Residential Care*, Oxford, Pergamon.

Ward, L. (1984) 'Keeping it Cool', *Social Work Today*, 15 (19), 17 January 1984.

Webb, D. (1976) 'Wise after the Event: some Comments on 'A Danger to Themselves and Others' ', *British Journal of Social Work*, 1976, 91–6.

Weller, M. (1984) 'Violence and Mental Illness', *British Medical Journal*, 289, 7 July 1984.

Wells, F. (1983) 'Assault', *British Medical Journal*, 286, 8 January 1983.

Whatmore, P. (1983) *Violence in Scottish Prisons*, Unpublished paper given at Inter-disciplinary Conference on Violence in the Individual, Portman Clinic, 28 September 1983.

Whitman, R. *et al.* (1976) 'Assault on the Therapist', *American Journal of Psychiatry*, 133, April 1976.

Wiener, R. (1983) 'When Emotions Overflow', *Community Care*, 458, 14 April 1983.

Williams, D. J. (1978) 'Acute Management of the Violent and Aggressive Patient', *Prescribers' Journal*, 18 (2), April 1978.

Woodman, D. (1979) 'Biochemical Cause for Violent Psychopathy?', *Psychology Today*, February 1979.

Woolfe, S. (1984) 'Thinking Physical', *Social Work Today*, 15 (46), 30 July 1984.

Videotape Training Materials

Violence – Its Prevention and Management, Robert Brown, Stanley Bute and Peter Ford, Hampshire Social Services Department and University of Southampton, 1982. Available from: Social Services Department, Archers House, 1A Archers Road, Southampton, Hampshire SO1 2LQ.

Handling Aggression and Conflict, East Sussex Consultancy and Training Agency, 1984. Available from: ESCATA, 6 Pavilion Parade, Brighton, East Sussex BN2 1RA.

Understanding and Handling Aggression, Malcolm Brown, Tavistock Publications, 1984. Available from: Associated Book Publishers (UK) Limited, North Way, Andover, Hampshire SP10 5BR.

INDEX